MAN
— VS. —
MARKETS

★ ★ ★

MAN

— VS. —

MARKETS

ECONOMICS EXPLAINED
(PLAIN AND SIMPLE)

PADDY HIRSCH

With Illustrations by Dan Archer

HARPER
BUSINESS

An Imprint of HarperCollins*Publishers*
www.harpercollins.com

HarperCollins books may be purchased for educational, business, or sales promotional use. For information, please e-mail the Special Markets Department, at SPsales@harpercollins.com.

FIRST EDITION

Designed by William Ruoto

Dan Archer creates nonfictional, journalistic comics (and occasional illustrations) to offer a new perspective on human rights issues and give voice to stories that wouldn't otherwise be heard. Read more of his work at www.archcomix.com.

Library of Congress Cataloging-in-Publication Data has been applied for.

ISBN: 978-0-06-219665-1

20 21 LSCH 10 9 8 7 6 5

ACKNOWLEDGMENTS

My thanks to everyone who made this book possible, particulary my wonderful agent, Laurie Fox at the Linda Chester Literary Agency, and my editor, Colleen Lawrie at HarperCollins. Thanks to Nancy Lilienthal, Darlene Chan, and Frank DePalma for introducing me to Laurie, and to Brandan Newman and Doug Krizner for their ideas, feedback, and support thoroughout the production process.

I owe a special debt to all the staff at Marketplace for their fellowship and friendship, and for their assistance with the creation of the Whiteboard, which showed me the need for this book. Dalasie Michaelis and Richard Core were instrumental in the Whiteboard's genesis—they had the idea of putting the first video on the Web, and Dalasie, Angela Kim, and Daryl Paranada have done a wonderful job of making me look good on camera over the years. Thanks also to JJ Yore for giving me the green light to take the Knight Fellowship, which gave me the time and mental bandwidth to produce the book.

Thank you to Kalika Nacion Yap for her invaluable help with my Web site and social media strategy, and to Monica Holloway and Michael Price for their unqualified and enthusiastic support and encouragement. Thanks also to Jim Bettinger, Dawn Garcia, Pam Maples, and all the staff and fellows of the 2011 Knight Fellowship. The year I spent with them at Stanford helped me see the world, and myself, in a different light, and gave me the resources that I needed to produce this book—not least by introducing me to the excellent comics journalist Dan Archer, whose illustrations adorn these pages.

Finally, and most importantly, thank you Eileen, for your love and consistent advice, and for putting the steel in my spine when I needed it most.

CONTENTS

What's that, you say? You don't need to understand the markets 'cause you're not *in* the markets? Oh. All right, then. Never mind about your 401(k). Or your teenager's college fund. Or the Treasury bond your Uncle Fred bought for the same teenager when she was born. You don't have a bank account? Or an insurance policy? Or a credit card? Or . . . well, I could continue but I think you see where I'm going.

While I'm at it, let's take care of one big misconception right up front. There is no such thing as "the market" (singular). When business journalists say, "Today the market reacted to . . . *blah blah blah*," it's actually quite the disservice. As the book you're about to read explains, "the markets" (plural) is a many-headed, often impenetrable, and frequently infuriating beast. Markets don't always work right. Sometimes they work all too well. Every now and then they simply stop working. (*see also*: Crash, financial, U.S., circa 2007–8.) But they matter. And we're stuck with them.

People often say the markets (plural) are basically gambling. That the odds are stacked against the average investor and he doesn't stand a chance. That's not entirely true. Yes, as you'll read, there are parts of the financial system where the house always wins. Sometimes it does always feel like everyone's betting against you. And, sure, professional speculators can always dislocate an otherwise rational trade. But day in and day out it's the money from those average investors—whether through retirement funds or home mortgages or any one of dozens of other trades—that makes the markets work.

One last thing—the title of this book is no accident. Investing *is* Man vs. Markets in the truest sense of the word. The markets (plural) aren't for the faint of heart. They're not for dabblers or casual passersby. They demand a certain degree of attention—never mind that you're not even *in* the markets (or so you think). You might not give a fig about the Dow Industrials or care what an option is, but believe me when I tell you what you don't know can hurt you—and what you learn in this book can help you immensely, no matter which path you take.

—Kai Ryssdal

The Financial Corner Store

A friend of mine—let's call him Tam—came to America from Southeast Asia as a young boy in the 1970s. He likes to tell the story of his family's first visit to the supermarket. He remembers walking into the store and encountering a dizzying array of produce in every color of the rainbow. He and his family were transfixed. They stood, staring at the rows and rows of fruits, vegetables, cans, and packages. They needed to buy groceries, but they were so bewildered by the endless variety of products in the store that they left without buying a thing.

The next day, Tam's mother went to the store with a neighbor, who showed her where to find the things the family was familiar with, and some new products that they would find useful. She taught them how to navigate the place, and how to find what they needed, pointing out familiar goods and suggesting alternatives to what they had used in their homeland. Pretty soon Mom, Dad, and all the kids knew the store as well as they knew their own home. And it wasn't long before they were complaining that the store, for all its variety, lacked products that had been staples in their country of origin.

Thank heaven for that friendly neighbor, who showed my friend's family there was nothing intimidating about the grocery store. In other words, she demystified that market.

Man vs. Markets aims to be just like that neighbor—a guide that will show you that the financial markets aren't as daunting as they might appear at first glance. In fact, when you look closely, a lot of what goes on in the markets is surprisingly familiar: most of what happens on Wall Street is actually a more involved version of what happens every day in billions of households all over the world.

When most people hear the word *market*, they immediately think about the **stock market**. That's because stocks, or **shares** in publicly traded companies, are the most high-profile investments in the financial world. They're a bit like apples at the grocery store: piled high in the center of the store and available all year round.

There are two interrelated reasons why shares are so prominent in the public consciousness. First, a huge number of Americans own them, either directly or through their retirement accounts. Perhaps as much as 50 percent of the U.S. population owns shares, according to studies by the Investment Company Institute. Second, because so many of us own stock, the media pays a great deal of attention to how those shares perform. That's why there's so much news coverage of movements in the Dow Jones Industrial Average or the S&P 500 here in the United States, the FTSE 100 in the United Kingdom, and the Nikkei 225 in Japan.

But just as there is a great deal more for sale in the grocery store than that pile of apples, there's a lot more available in the financial markets than just shares. Bonds, futures, swaps, money market funds, collateralized debt obligations, currencies: in the financial markets, exotic products are piled high by bankers who are constantly looking for new things to sell to investors.

Man vs. Markets will walk you up and down the aisles. It'll explain what each product is doing on the shelf, how it's created, and how it works. By the end, you'll have a much better idea of how the markets function, who's buying what, and why. Like Tam's family, you'll soon be able to tell which products are safe, which are risky, and how to identify all of the market's shortcomings.

MAN
— vs. —
MARKETS

★ ★ ★

CHAPTER ONE

Your Piece of the Action

Stocks, Shares, and Equity Trading

In an ideal world, a company opens its doors, starts making products, attracts customers, and the money rolls in. But it doesn't always happen this way, and companies often find they need to get money from somewhere outside the company—from **investors**.

There are essentially two ways for investors to put money into a company. They can either buy a share of it, or they can lend money to it.

Most of us recall the story of the "Three Little Pigs." The three porcine brothers each built a house: one of straw, one of wood, and one of brick. In the Disney version of the story, the big bad wolf made short work of the first two houses, and sent their owners running to the third brother, in the solid brick house. What we glean from the ending is that the brother welcomed them in and offered them shelter from the wolf.

But I bet the third brother—let's call him Cuthbert—didn't let his siblings, Dibble and Grub, come live with him without getting something in return. That brick house took time, effort, and money to build! Cuthbert had to take out a loan to pay for the materials and all that chipmunk labor, which meant he had an interest payment to make each month. Here's how I imagine the porcine brothers talking about the house:

CUTHBERT: If you're going to live here, you're going to have to pay your way.

DIBBLE: You mean pay rent?

CUTHBERT: No, I don't trust either of you deadbeats to come up with the money every month.

GRUB: So what then?

CUTHBERT: It cost me $6,000 to build this house. If you split the cost with me, and pay me $2,000 each, you can live here as long as you like. We'll decide together what kind of maintenance and upkeep the place needs as we go, and we'll split those costs.

DIBBLE: So we can live with you here, safe from the wolf, forever . . . for just $2,000 flat, plus a monthly maintenance fee?

CUTHBERT: That's about the size of it, yes.

DIBBLE AND GRUB (IN UNISON): It's a deal!

And with that, the three little pigs became **shareholders** in the brick house.

A **share** is as simple as that—a part ownership of something, also known as **stocks**, or as an **equity stake**.

You can hold equity stakes in anything: homes, cars, a painting, companies—the list is endless.

And it's easy to do: Let's imagine I decide to go into the ice cream business together with my friend Linda. We split the cost of an ice cream van, and all the equipment and supplies. The result is that Linda and I become equal shareholders in our business: we each own an equity stake of 50 percent.

Billions of people own stock in companies: In March 2010, the *New York Times* reported that roughly half of all Americans own shares. But there are two important differences between those shares and the ones owned by the three little pigs, or the shares my friend and I have in our ice cream truck. For one, the shares most Americans own are in **publicly traded companies**, not private enterprises like Linda's and mine. And they're usually tiny slivers of the entire worth of the firm, not stakes of 50 percent.

How do private companies become public? And why are their shares such tiny slices of the company's worth?

Let's take a closer look at my ice cream business—let's call it **Jolliwhip**. At first, Jolliwhip is a private company, with two owners, Linda and me. Over the years, we become very large and successful. One day we decide to buy out a competitor, but we haven't got enough money. We have essentially two options: we can either get a loan or raise the money by selling a share of our company for cash.

Unfortunately, that's hard to do when you have only two shares, each worth 50 percent. It's far easier to sell a small piece of a company. So, to make Jolliwhip easier to divide up, we split it into a *million* shares. Now we still each own half of the company, but that means we have half a million shares each.

Our plan is to sell 80 percent of Jolliwhip, or 800,000 shares, and each keep 10 percent, or 100,000 shares for ourselves. Again we have a number of options. We can sell that 80 percent stake to a private investor or investors. If we do this, we'll remain a private company, and our buyers will be considered **private equity** investors.

Our other option is to **go public,** or become a publicly traded company. In this scenario, we're still selling chunks of Jolliwhip to investors, but we're doing it through the open market, to people we don't know and will probably never meet.

THE EAST INDIA COMPANIES ➤

The first companies to sell shares were European trading firms that sent ships to India and Asia in the sixteenth and seventeenth centuries. Investors lent money to fund individual voyages at first, but it was a risky business: ships were often lost at sea, and many investors lost money. So it was tough to find people willing to come up with the cash that captains needed to equip their ships and pay their crews.

In 1599 British shipowners clubbed together to form a single organization, the East India Company. People who bought shares in this new company now invested in every voyage, rather than in individual ships.

Periodically, they were paid a share of the company's profits for as long as they held their shares. Shares that they could then sell to someone else if they wished, of course!

When big companies go public, they **list** their shares on an **exchange**, like the NASDAQ and the New York Stock Exchange. To get that listing, companies have to have a track record, be a certain size, and make a certain amount of money. Smaller companies are traded in what's called the **over-the-counter** market. A company choosing an exchange is a bit like a beekeeper, who can sell her honey either through a superstore or at the local street market. The store has all sorts of standards and checks that the honey has to pass to make it onto the shelves. And the beekeeper has to be able to guarantee the honey supply to keep the contract. Exchanges, like superstores, are highly regulated and have all sorts of requirements. When you're selling from a street stall—or in the over-the-counter market, in the case of shares—there are many fewer controls. So it's a lot simpler to sell on the street, or over the counter. The downside is, you get a lot fewer customers. If you want a lot of people buying your stuff, then you're better off being in a place where many more people are shopping. Which is why most beekeepers would love to get a deal with a supermarket, and why companies usually aspire to be listed on an exchange.

A market, then, is simply a place where people come together to buy and sell stuff, whether it be honey or shares. It can be a physical market, like your local flea market, or the floor of the New York Stock Exchange; or it can be an electronic market, like eBay, or the Kansas City–based share market BATS. A market can be public, like the NYSE, which is shown on television every day, or it can be private, involving just two people. And some people do enjoy private transactions, like buying things through Craigslist. But most of us prefer to buy and sell in a more open market.

If you want to transact on eBay, for example, you can see how much similar items have sold for in the recent past. This is called **transparency**, and it means knowing as much as possible about something, perhaps most important about price. When people buy honey at a market, they prefer to know what everyone else is paying. If they don't know, they're a lot less likely to buy. Most people would hesitate to buy honey from a stall where there are no prices displayed and everyone is being charged a different price based on their relationship to the seller. The same goes for shares: buyers want to shop where shares are trading all the time, and where prices are clearly displayed. If they can't find out the price of a share quickly and easily, they're unlikely to buy anything at all. That's why exchanges make a point of always being up-to-date when they display their share prices.

Unarguably, transparency is good for buyers in any market: they can see how much each seller is charging and can shop around for the best price. Transparency benefits sellers, too: people are more likely to do business in a transparent market where they can trust they're not getting ripped off. And it helps sellers when they can see their competitors' prices: they can price their own wares more accurately.

Transparency, accurate pricing, and competition between sellers attracts buyers. Buyers attract sellers, and the more buyers and sellers that come together, the easier it is to buy or sell a stock. Financial people call this **liquidity**—a **liquid market** being one where trading takes place smoothly and quickly. The market is a bit like a hall where couples strut traditional dances like tangos and waltzes that require someone to lead and a partner to follow. A person who likes to lead wants to go where she knows she'll find lots of people willing to follow—to a liquid market for her dancing skills. Conversely, a person who likes to follow wants to go dancing in a place where she'll find people willing to lead. When lots of leaders and followers come together, the hall becomes filled with dancers, all waltzing away.

But if most of the people in the hall want to lead, and there are only a few followers, we have an **illiquid market**, with only a few couples on the floor, and a lot of leaders hanging out on the sidelines, hoping for a follower to dance with. The dancers, of course, are the buyers and sellers on either side of a securities transaction, and the hall they dance in is the exchange.

At this point, it's worth explaining the difference between an exchange, like the NYSE and the NASDAQ, and an **index**, like the Dow Jones Industrial Average, or the Standard & Poor's 500. An exchange is a place you go to buy and sell shares. An index, on the other hand, is just a list of company shares that can come from a variety of different exchanges.

Most big establishments have goods that are only sold in their stores, like the Organics line sold by Safeway, or Trader Joe's store-brand products. Exchanges work the same way: the shares that are bought and sold on an exchange can only be traded on those exchanges. An index, on the other hand, is merely a list of the "biggest" products that trade on all sorts of different exchanges. The Dow consists of thirty of the biggest companies traded in the United States, some of which trade on the NYSE, others of which trade on the NASDAQ. The S&P 500 index is a list of five hundred of the most actively traded companies on the NYSE and the NASDAQ.

Imagine if someone decided to build a list of the biggest-selling store-brand products from Safeway, Whole Foods, Kroger, and Piggly Wiggly. You could track their collective sales performance throughout the day and reflect it on a graph. That's exactly what the people who run indices like the Dow do; only they do it with shares of companies, instead of bags of sugar and loaves of bread. So when you hear reporters and analysts refer to the Dow or the S&P being up or down, it's those graphs they're talking about. Investors can use indices to gauge the performance of the whole market, or only of certain parts of the market. For example, the Dow and the S&P focus on big companies, the NASDAQ 100 index tracks technology firms, while the Russell 2000 index is composed of small firms. It helps to think of the entire market as a body, and the indices like the readings from a thermometer. Stick the thermometer in the center of the body and you'll get a different reading than if you measured the temperature of a hand or a foot. Which is why the Wilshire 5000, which takes into account the performance of almost every stock in the market, has a different reading to the tech-heavy Goldman Sachs Technology Index Semiconductor Index, for example.

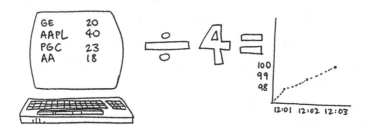

Take a close look at pretty much any index and you'll see that the line that tracks the performance of the index over time is rarely straight. Usually it jumps up and down, and sometimes it can look like a roller-coaster ride. When the ride looks particularly bumpy, financiers say the market is **volatile**. **Volatility** often occurs when there aren't many people trading, perhaps because a market is illiquid, or because people are on vacation. In our dance hall, that would mean those couples that were dancing would have the whole floor to themselves, so they could swing and cavort back

and forth, using the whole place to waltz about. In a full hall, however, it's a lot more difficult to let loose. The dancers are confined, only able to move in a small range.

In a market, if only a few people are trading, the number of shares bought and sold—also known as the trading **volume**—falls. Low trading volume makes it easier for traders to influence the direction of a share or even an index, just as low attendance in a dance hall makes it easier for couples to move around.

Volume isn't the only factor governing volatility. Emotion plays its part, too. There's a saying in the financial markets that there are really only two emotions in trading: fear and greed. And depending on which one holds sway at any given time, the market will rise or fall. If people think a company's in trouble, fear overwhelms them, and they sell. If they think they're getting a bargain, greed kicks in, and they buy.

Human beings aren't just emotional; they're easily influenced, too. When we see people running down a street in a panic, the natural reaction is to join the crowd, not go against the flow. The same goes for many investors. When they see people selling a company's shares, they think, "There must be something wrong!" and they sell. When they see other people buying, they buy. Not all investors behave this way, however. Good investors take time to do their homework, to determine whether a company's shares are properly priced. Good homework helps them decide whether to follow the herd or go against it. It also helps them decide whether a share is likely to rise or fall, and therefore whether to go **long** or **short**.

Short sellers borrow shares and sell them in the hope that the price will fall. When it does, they buy the shares back at the lower price—called **covering** the short—return the shares to the original owner—called **closing the position**—and pocket the difference.

THE LONG AND SHORT OF IT ➤

Long and **short** are terms that securities traders use to describe their intentions.

"I'm long Apple" means you intend to buy Apple securities, hold them for a comparatively long time, and then sell after they have gained in price. You're betting they'll rise, in other words.

"I'm short AT&T" means you're betting AT&T securities will fall. You make money on this bet by **selling short**.

Dibble, the middle of our three porcine brothers, is an old hand at shorting. In fact he started with baseball cards when he was a piglet.

> **DIBBLE:** Hey, Cuthbert, lend me your Roger Maris card.
> **CUTHBERT:** Okay. But I want it back by the end of next month, for the convention.
> **DIBBLE:** No problem, brah.
> **CUTHBERT:** Don't call me that. It's irritating.

That afternoon, Dibble meets his buddy Julio in the park.

DIBBLE: Hey, Julio, I got that Roger Maris card you wanted. It's yours for fifteen bucks, my friend.

JULIO: I'm pretty sure you're working an angle here, Dibble, but I'll give you ten.

DIBBLE: Deal.

That night, watching the game . . .

CUTHBERT: Hey, can I see my Maris card for a second?

DIBBLE: I haven't got it.

CUTHBERT: What do you mean? Where is it?

DIBBLE: I sold it.

CUTHBERT: You sold it?! That's my only Roger Maris card!

DIBBLE: Relax! Either Mark McGwire or Sammy Sosa is gonna break that home run record in the next few days, and then Maris cards are gonna be two a penny. You wait, brah!

CUTHBERT: Didn't I tell you to stop calling me that?

Sure enough, both McGwire and Sosa set home run records. Two days later, Dibble meets Julio in the park.

JULIO: My man Dibble! Can I interest you in Roger Clemens for $8?

DIBBLE: Trying to raise the $20 for one of those Sosa cards, huh? Tell you what, I'll give you five bucks for that Roger Maris card I sold you yesterday.

JULIO: Five bucks? I *knew* you were working some angle! Okay, it's a deal. Hand over the cash!

Dibble goes home and returns the card to Cuthbert. The remaining $5 he keeps for himself.

All's well when the card market goes Dibble's way. But what if Sammy Sosa and Mark McGwire hadn't made those home runs? What if the value of the Roger Maris card then rises to $20? Most traders who short stock borrow their shares from a broker, with the shares acting as collateral. When the share price rises, the traders lose money on paper—Dibble, for example, is down $10 on paper now that the Roger Maris card is worth $20. When traders are **out of the money**, their brokers get nervous, and they often ask the traders to post more collateral.

CUTHBERT: So much for your fortune-telling skills. Looks like everybody still loves Roger Maris! I saw Julio today. He says it's gonna cost you $15 to buy my card back. Maybe even $20.

DIBBLE: I'll get it back, I promise.

CUTHBERT: Maybe you will, maybe you won't. Either way, I want some security. Give me ten bucks to hold, and I'll give it back to you when you give me my card.

If the trader has spare cash lying around, it's easy to meet the broker's **collateral call**, as it's called. If not, the trader has to **close out the position** by buying back the shares at the higher price.

DIBBLE: But I haven't got $10, brah.

CUTHBERT: Then I suggest you dial the seven digits and find a way to get my card off Julio while it's still comparatively cheap . . . brah.

> DIBBLE: Hey, Julio. Sorry to call you so late, but I need to buy that card off you. . . . What? Twenty-five bucks? You're joking! . . . Wait, okay, okay. Twenty-five it is.

MARGIN OF ERROR ➤

Many traders borrow money from brokers to buy shares, betting that they'll rise in price.

This is called trading on **margin**, and it comes with risks as big as those associated with selling short.

If the share price falls, the brokers worry they might not get their money back. So they demand more collateral—usually in the form of cash or other securities. This is called a **margin call**.

Margin calls can drive share prices down sharply, as traders sell shares for no other reason than to make the money they need to pay their debts.

Heavy demand from short sellers who've bet the wrong way can trigger a chain reaction called a **short squeeze**: the demand for the stock drives the price higher, and brokers respond by insisting on more collateral from other short sellers. They, in turn, may have to buy the stock. That demand drives the stock price higher still, and so on. The more people who were betting the stock would fall, the tighter the squeeze.

Naked shorts "sell" shares without borrowing them first. Imagine if Cuthbert had refused to lend Dibble the card.

> DIBBLE: Hey, Julio, I can sell you that Roger Maris card for $10.
>
> JULIO: Okay. Here's the cash. Where's the card?

DIBBLE: My brother's on a field trip. He'll be back in three days. I'll have it to you then, promise.

JULIO: You're working some kind of angle again, I can feel it. But okay. If you don't give it up, then I'll tell my brother, and then you'll be sorry.

Julio hands over the cash. Three days later, McGwire and Sosa are on top, and Dibble's able to buy the Roger Maris card from another buddy for $5. He gives the card to Julio, as promised, and pockets the leftover $5. Phew! If the market had moved the other way, he'd have been chasing Roger Maris cards all over town and paying through the snout to make good on his promise to Julio!

Most of the shares that are traded on exchanges and listed on indexes are called **ordinary shares**, or **common stock**. But while the shares may be ordinary, the people who own them get extraordinary treatment.

For one thing, a common stockholder usually has the right to vote on decisions made by the company board, even if he or she owns just one share. For another, ordinary shareholders are often paid a **dividend**, which is a portion of the money a company makes. If the Jolliwhip ice cream company makes a profit, I can either reinvest that money in the firm or I can divvy it up and pay my shareholders. Paying dividends is a way of repaying an investor's faith in a company, and it helps to push the price of the shares higher in the market. Not every company's shares come with a dividend, but investors love dividends, so many companies do their best to pay them.

Ordinary shares are called "ordinary" (or common) to distinguish them from **preferred** stock or shares. Preferred shares are traded on exchanges, and they often come with a higher dividend. But their name is a bit of a red herring because they aren't really shares at all—at least, they don't represent slices of a company in the way common shares do.

I like to think of preferred shares as the fancy scrollwork we often see grafted under the roof or around the windows of an old building. It looks great and may add to the value of the place, but we could chip it off and toss it away, and the building itself would be unaffected: that scrollwork is not part of the building's essential structure.

On the other hand, the building's bricks *are* essential. And in the same way that the sum of the bricks that make up a building *are* the building, the sum of a company's ordinary shares *is* the company. Companies make money by selling ownership of those bricks—those shares—to investors. The problem is, of course, that there are only so many bricks to sell, but financiers have come up with some creative ways to cope with that particular problem, as the continuing tale of the "Three Little Pigs" (director's cut) will show.

Cuthbert, Dibble, and Grub, are now living comfortably in their brick house. Each now has a certificate saying they own a third of the property, which makes the two younger brothers feel rather safe and smug. Now that they're landowners, they figure, they only need to work part-time jobs, and they've got into the habit of lazing about the place.

Dibble has also taken to gambling in the evenings, and one morning, he saunters into the kitchen, looking a little sheepish (which is very odd, for a pig).

DIBBLE:	Got some bad news I'm afraid, lads. Lost a bit of money last night.
GRUB:	So what's new? How much did you lose this time?
DIBBLE:	A thousand bucks.
CUTHBERT AND GRUB **(IN UNISON):**	*What!?*

DIBBLE:	Yeah, it's bad, I know.

CUTHBERT: Please tell me you didn't use a marker.

GRUB: What's a marker?

CUTHBERT: It's the amount you borrow from the house.

GRUB: Yeah, please tell us you didn't use a marker, Dibble!

DIBBLE: Sorry, lads. I owe the whole thousand. I figure the only way I can pay my marker is to sell my share in the house.

CUTHBERT: No way. Absolutely not. You can't go back to living in that straw hut! The wolf will just blow it down, and we'll be in no position to save your bacon.

DIBBLE: Very droll, smart guy. So what do we do?

CUTHBERT: We bring in another investor.

GRUB: But we only have three shares. And I'm not selling mine.

CUTHBERT: No, we **split** the shares. As of now, instead of each having one share worth $2,000, we each have two shares worth $1,000 apiece.

DIBBLE: I get it! So I can just sell one of the shares and pay off my marker! And I'll still have one share.

CUTHBERT: Which means you'll still be able to live here.

DIBBLE: Wow! Thanks, Cuthbert!

GRUB: So whoever buys the share'll be in Dibble's room, right?

The three little pigs have done what in a public company is called a **stock split**. Public companies split their stocks when they want to create a greater number of individual shares to sell to the public, but without changing the value of each investor's holding. This can be useful if the share price before the split was very high. If the price of an individual share is lower, it's likely easier to sell, as smaller investors can afford to buy

in at the lower price. Some companies split their stock in the hope that the shares will rise in value because those smaller investors are now able to buy more easily. But there's no guarantee this will happen.

Fortunately, the three little pigs aren't interested in boosting the value of their home. They are, however, interested in finding a way to get rid of their new investor. Thor is a smelly old porker who snores so loudly that Dibble is forced to sleep in Grub's room. Worst of all, he drinks the communal milk straight out of the carton, which drives Cuthbert crazy. One day, when Thor is out at work, Cuthbert calls a conference.

CUTHBERT:	It's the last straw. That disgusting old boar took a bite out of my leftover pastrami sandwich, then put it back in the fridge! I've had enough. We're getting rid of him.
GRUB:	How? He's huge! And he's got those enormous tusks!
CUTHBERT:	Don't worry about that. I'm going to make life so unpleasant for him that he won't want to stay. I'm going to **dilute his share**!
DIBBLE:	What does that mean?
CUTHBERT:	It means I'm going to create a bunch more shares and sell them to other investors.

GRUB: You mean, another split?

CUTHBERT: No. This time, we issue shares on top of the shares we already have. Another six shares, to be precise.

DIBBLE: Aha! So now there will be 12 shares in the house.

GRUB: What does that mean?

CUTHBERT: Well, right now, our house is worth $6,000, and there are 6 shares, so each share is worth $1,000. When we issue these new shares, each share will be worth just $500.

GRUB: Do we get more shares?

CUTHBERT: Not unless you buy them.

GRUB: So what you're telling me is, my share will be worth half what it is now, and we could have another six pigs living here?

CUTHBERT: That's the plan.

When Thor returns that evening, Cuthbert announces that because they need money to fix the leaking roof and a hole in the chimney, they have to sell six more shares. Thor is not happy, as he knows **share dilution** when he sees it, but Cuthbert puts it to a vote and the three little pigs raise their trotters.

A week later, six student piglets move in. They come and go at all hours and keep some very strange things in the fridge. It's too much for Thor, who's angry at having the value of his share cut in half and furious at having to share a room. One day he corners Cuthbert and demands that the three pigs buy him out for the original price of a thousand dollars a share.

CUTHBERT: Four hundred.

THOR: Eight hundred.

CUTHBERT: Five.

THOR:	Seven.
CUTHBERT:	Six.
THOR:	Six-fifty.
CUTHBERT:	Done.

And with that, Thor is gone.

The practice of **share dilution** is common in the business world. Cuthbert did so by selling shares in what's called a **secondary offering**. A secondary offering gives the company access to more money, but leaves the company vulnerable to a number of pitfalls. Existing investors hate seeing any kind of reduction in the value of their investments. And share dilution can also damage a company in the eyes of potential investors, who keep a close eye on something called **earnings per share**, or **EPS**. They obtain this figure by calculating the amount the company earns in a year and dividing that sum by the number of shares. Investors are tantalized when they see a nice fat EPS number, but more important, they are thrilled when see that number grow over time. And dilution makes EPS shrink.

For example, if the pigs ran a little accounting business out of their house and made 60,000 a year, their EPS before the secondary offering would have been 10,000 (that's 60,000, divided by 6 shares). After the offering, their EPS is 5,000. Not so attractive, even to an old boar like Thor.

If companies feel that a secondary offering will dilute their investors' shares too much or damage their profile in the eyes of the market, they'll look for other ways to raise the money they need. Wall Street bankers have come up with all sorts of inventive ways to coax cash from investors—preferred shares are a good example—but perhaps the most popular method of raising money is the oldest and simplest of all: borrowing.

CHAPTER TWO

Racking It Up

Debt, and Why It's Not Always a Bad Thing

Debt, or **leverage**, as it's often called, got a bad name during the financial crisis of 2008–10, when the whole world got a nasty taste of what happens if a company borrows too much.

But just because some people overdid it doesn't mean that all borrowing is bad. Have you ever heard the phrase "His ship came in"? It refers to someone who gets a windfall or cashes in on an investment. This adage dates to the fifteenth century, when an investor would finance a trading voyage to India or beyond. Some investors risked their own money, but others borrowed heavily, hoping the ship would return stuffed with spices, silks, and precious stones that would fetch a huge profit. Many of these ships disappeared on the high seas without a trace, but if the ship did eventually come in to its home port, the investor would rejoice, sell the cargo—and pay off his debt.

Indeed, borrowing money is one of the oldest engines of economic growth. If business owners hadn't been able to borrow, the great trading fleets of Britain, China, Portugal, Arabia, and Spain, to name but a few, would never have been launched, the engineers of the industrial revolution would never have been financed, and the medicines and surgical technology that save so many lives today would never have been created.

Right now, my company, Jolliwhip, consists of an ice cream manufacturing facility and a bunch of trucks. Let's imagine, however, that one day, a local ice cream parlor goes up for sale. The owner is retiring and wants to offload the property. The parlor is a successful business with lots of potential: it's close to the beach and several schools, and it has a loyal clientele. In fact it's a real moneymaker, and Linda and I know that if we bought it and set up shop, we could raise enough money to buy the new equipment our manufacturing facility needs.

But the sad truth is, Linda and I don't have enough cash to buy that ice cream parlor. And we don't want to sell shares in *our* company; we like running it the way we run it now. Which means the only way to raise the cash we need to buy the parlor is to borrow.

There are a number of ways to borrow money. We could max out our credit cards. We could refinance our respective houses and pull cash out of the newly inflated mortgage. We could ask our parents to lend us money. We could go to a bank or a credit union and ask for a loan. And if we're big enough, we could go to the **bond** market.

These methods of financing sound different and are labeled differently, but they are basically the same in that they are all various types of debt. And debt is debt, whether you're a company borrowing money from a bank or a child borrowing a toy from a friend.

Most of us learn how to go into debt before we can even walk. If you doubt this, take a close look at children playing in a schoolyard. The kids having the most fun are doing what every good parent encourages her child to do more than anything else: share. When children share with each other, they make friends, socialize, and mature as human beings. The child that refuses to share runs the risk of ending up friendless, isolated, antisocial, and emotionally stunted.

No parent would argue that sharing is a bad thing. And yet sharing is nothing more than borrowing and lending. Angela learns quickly that

OBLIGATION   CONTRACT

she can't simply take Jimmy's toy truck if she likes the look of it. Jimmy has to agree to hand it over, and Angela has to agree to give it back.

Children learn very quickly what an **obligation** is: Jimmy agrees to share his truck with the understanding that Angela is obliged to return it. Angela is also aware of her obligation. It's a **contract**, the breach of which is likely to end in tears—and often does.

Which brings us to the other thing about debt that kids learn quickly: human beings have a tendency to renege on their agreements and default on their obligations!

Which is where that most basic of written loan agreements materializes: the **IOU**.

The Loan

It's the first Monday back at school after the holidays, and Kim has brought with her the present she got from her grandma. In the past, grandma had bought Kim a box of one hundred Hershey bars, but this year she decided Kim needed to exercise more often, so she bought her a jump rope instead.

And what a jump rope it is! It's made of multicolored, strengthened nylon, and it has those rotating ball-bearing handles, so it turns easily and makes it simpler to do tricks. Kim draws quite a crowd in the

playground, showing off her skills with her new toy, until another child, Tony, approaches her.

TONY: Hey, Kim, I like your jump rope. It's very cool!

KIM: Thanks.

TONY: Will you trade it for some candy?

KIM: You can't afford that much candy. My grandma usually gives me 100 Hershey bars for the holidays, so the way I see it, that's what this rope is worth: 100 candy bars.

TONY: You're right, I can't afford that. But can I borrow your rope until Friday to try it out? Then, if I like it, I can ask my dad to buy one for me.

KIM: Okay, but it'll cost you.

TONY: How much?

KIM: One Hershey bar a day.

Tony agrees, and writes up an IOU:

An IOU is just a piece of paper, but in the financial world, **paper** is a powerful term: it's often used as a generic term for debt in place of words such as loan or bond.

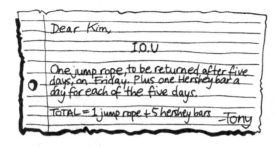

Tony's IOU represents an agreement with Kim, and Tony's obligation to pay her back. It outlines the terms of the loan, including the **principal** (the jump rope); the **term** of the loan (five days); its **maturity** date (Friday); and a fixed **interest rate** and **payment schedule** (one Hershey bar to be paid each day). It's just like a **term sheet**, which is what bankers call the document they draw up when they make loans to people and to companies.

Anyone who has ever borrowed from a bank has heard all of these words before, but there's another term used by banks in the lending business that may not be as familiar: **yield**.

Yield is a word that makes many people think of farming and the crop yields that wheat and corn growers report after the harvest. A farmer sows a ton of wheat grain in her field, then waits. If all goes well, the wheat grows and ripens and, within a few months, is ready to harvest. Once the harvest is in, the farmer finds herself with three tons of grain. Those three tons are the crop's **yield**.

Lenders are a bit like farmers; only the seed they sow is money. They make loans and reap "harvests" in the form of regular interest payments from the borrower. This is where lenders stop looking like farmers and begin to appear more complicated. The yields that lenders deal with come in several different forms, so we'll address the simplest and most common: **nominal yield**. Nominal yield is the amount of **interest income** a lender harvests from a loan over a certain period. It is usually expressed as a percentage of the original loan.

Take Kim and Tony's loan. Here's how a banker would calculate its nominal yield:

Principal:	1 jump rope (valued at 100 Hershey bars)
Term:	5 days
Maturity:	Friday afternoon
Interest:	1 Hershey bar, to be paid daily, for 5 days
Nominal Yield (daily):	(1 Hershey Bar ÷ 100 Hershey bars) x 100 = 1 percent

Nominal yield on our home loans or school loans is calculated in exactly the same way, only on an annual basis. Which is why many people in the lending business call nominal yield the **annual percentage rate**, or APR.

Wow! It's easy to see, just from reading the last paragraph, why most people feel so helpless when they cross paths with the financial services industry. There's so much jargon and so many interchangeable terms for the simplest things, such as loans or interest rates.

That's why it's especially important to pay close attention to the paperwork that a bank gives you when you borrow a loan, and to understand the bank's language. All the information you need will be in the loan documents, but unfortunately it won't be laid out as clearly and simply as in Tony and Kim's IOU agreement. So you may need a little assist with the translation. The most important thing is to understand the extent of your obligation. Strip out the jargon and the loan document becomes an IOU: it tells you what you have to pay and when. And signing an IOU or a loan document is no small matter. You're making a legally binding agreement with a moral commitment to pay. When Tony signs his scrap of paper and gives it to Kim, he's giving her his word that he'll pay her back with interest. And, to quote from the Latin: *dictum meum pactum*.

My word is my bond.

The Bond

A bond, like a loan, is simply a promise to pay a sum of money. In fact, certain types of bonds are called **promissory notes** (notes, or pieces of paper, bearing a promise to pay). The person who is borrowing the money is called the **bond issuer**. The lender is called the **bondholder** because he is holding the borrower's promise to pay.

A bond looks a lot like a loan agreement on the surface. It includes the amount that the bondholder has lent, the maturity date of the bond, and the interest rate—also known in the trade as the **coupon**.

There's a significant difference in the way loans and bonds are created. If Linda and I want to expand Jolliwhip, we can obtain a loan by simply meeting with the bank manager. She will look at our books and decide on the amount she's prepared to lend and what our interest rate will be.

Going to the bond market is far more complicated. Most loans are agreements between a borrower and a single lender, but bonds often involve multiple lenders.

If Linda and I want to obtain money from the bond market, we have to go on a bond **roadshow**. A roadshow is akin to a string of bank manager meetings, except the people listening to our pitch and deciding whether or not to lend us money aren't just banks, they're also investment companies such as pension funds. Based on how much each investor intimates he'll lend us, and at what price (and this can vary greatly), we get an idea of how many bonds we'll need to sell and what interest rate we'll need to pay. This process is called **pricing** the bonds.

Once we come up with an interest rate that the investors find agreeable, we can go ahead and sell, or **issue**, the bonds. Financiers say the bonds are sold in the **primary market**, because it's the first time they're sold to anyone. Each investor receives a piece of paper, just like Kim and Tony's IOU, stating that they've lent me a certain amount at a certain rate for a certain period. In return, the investors give us the amount of money stated on the bond, also called the bond's **face value**.

Our investors are now free to do whatever they like with that bond. They can hold it, which means tucking it into their vault and collecting interest until the bond matures. Or they can sell the bond in what's called the **secondary market**.

It's in the secondary market that most of the confusion about bonds and loans arises, mainly in the relationship between the bond or loan's price and its yield.

For example, consider the loan that Kim made to Tony. She lent him one jump rope; he gave her a piece of paper. That piece of paper—call it a bond or a loan document or an IOU—gives her the right to one Hershey bar a day, plus a jump rope come Friday. Now, if she likes, Kim can hand that piece of paper over to anyone who wants it—and the person who's holding the paper will now get the candy bars and the rope.

Kim's classmate Mandy has been watching Kim and Tony's exchange and is intrigued by the transaction they have struck. Mandy has a brand-new jump rope, too, and she dearly loves chocolate. Boy, does she wish she had done a deal like that with her rope!

Suddenly, she has an idea:

MANDY: Hey, Kim, I heard you lent your jump rope to Tony. Aren't you worried that he'll break it?

KIM: Well, I'm getting one Hershey bar a day in exchange for lending it.

MANDY: But I know how much you love to jump rope. Won't you miss it?

KIM: I guess so.

MANDY: Why don't you take my rope? It's exactly the
              same as yours. If Tony breaks yours, then I'll be
              the one without a rope, not you.

KIM: What about the Hershey bars?

MANDY: Well, I'd be the one taking the risk, so he'd give
              the chocolate to me, right?

Kim takes a moment to consider Mandy's proposal. She imagines
Tony using her rope to tie up his little brother and then having to cut him
loose with a knife! Maybe it wouldn't be so bad to give up the chocolate
after all. But Kim still has a sweet tooth that needs satisfying—is there a
way she can still get just a little chocolate out of the deal?

KIM: How much chocolate do you have on you right
              now?

MANDY: Half a Hershey bar.

KIM: Okay. If you give me the candy right now, you
              can have this IOU.

Mandy pulls her jump rope out of her bag, along with half a Hershey bar, and hands it to Kim. Kim crosses out her own name on the IOU, substitutes Mandy's name, and hands the piece of paper over to Mandy.

Now Kim has a skipping rope, and half a candy bar to satisfy her short-term chocolate craving. Mandy has Tony's bond, which means she'll get a candy bar from Tony every day, and come Friday she'll have a skipping rope, too—hopefully in one piece.

The Yield

Mandy might have persuaded Kim to exchange the IOU for Mandy's jump rope and nothing more. In other words, paying the same price for the IOU as Kim did. This is called paying **par**, or 100 percent of the original price of the bond. But Mandy is paying a little bit more than par. The price of the bond has changed—it was originally one jump rope, but now it's one jump rope plus half a Hershey bar—and that means the **current yield** on the bond has also changed. This is a different kind of yield to the nominal yield we mentioned earlier. Nominal yield was the yield on the bond when it was first priced and sold. The current yield is the yield on the bond when it trades in the market.

The Math

At this point it's useful for Mandy to go back and review the "term sheet" of Tony's IOU.

Principal:	1 jump rope (value 100 Hershey bars)
Term:	5 days
Maturity:	Friday afternoon
Interest:	1 Hershey bar, daily, for 5 days
Nominal Yield (daily):	(interest rate ÷ face value) x 100
(1 Hershey bar ÷ 100 Hershey bars) x 100 = 1 percent	

The nominal yield of Tony's bond is 1 percent; it is calculated using the face value of the bond. The *current* yield is calculated using the bond's current value in the market, or in other words, what people are paying for the bond. Kim paid the full face value of the bond, so the current yield at that point was the same as the nominal yield: 1 percent.

But Mandy paid more! She gave Kim a jump rope (equal to 100 Hershey bars) *plus* half a Hershey bar of her own. Which means the price of the bond was 100.5.

As far as Tony is concerned, nothing changes: he still pays interest of one Hershey bar, or 1 percent, a day. But Mandy isn't getting quite as good a deal as Kim did. The yield on the bond has now fallen: if she divides the interest (1 bar) by the price (100.5 bars) she now gets 0.009, or *less than* 1 percent.

Current Yield (daily): (interest rate ÷ face value) x 100
(1 Hershey Bar ÷ 100.5 Hershey bars) x 100 = 0.9 percent

There's no way Mandy would be able to save every one of the five Hershey bars Tony pays her until the end of the week. But if she did, she'd see that, because she paid half a bar to Kim up front, she will net just four and a half bars, whereas Kim would have netted the full five bars.

Yields can go up as well as down. If Tony's using Kim's brand-new rope to play tug-of-war, when Mandy makes her offer, Kim might be willing to take a ratty old skipping rope in return for the IOU, figuring it's better to have an old but intact rope now, rather than risk receiving a broken and useless one in a week's time.

In this case, Mandy's investment pays off substantially: her raggedy old piece of string has yielded a nearly brand-new jump rope plus an additional five chocolate bars! If we assume the ratty rope is worth 50 candy bars, that's a yield-to-maturity of 55 bars, or 155 percent, which will taste pretty sweet to Mandy.

Whatever happens in the secondary market that's being held on the school playground, it's all the same to Tony. The IOU that he gave to Kim in return for the loan of her jump rope could change hands a hundred times, and it would make no difference to him (except that he'd have to keep track of to whom to pay Hershey bars). His bond could trade back and forth all day long, but the amount that he owes remains constant throughout.

LENDING THROUGH THE AGES ➤

Debt instruments have been around for a lot longer than stocks. Historians have found references to moneylenders in ancient Indian manuscripts, dating back to 2000 BC.

Greek and Roman philosophers, including Plato, Aristotle, Cicero, and Seneca, all wrote about moneylenders—and rarely in flattering terms. The Jewish Talmud, the Muslim Quran, and the Christian Bible all condemn usury, which can be interpreted either as lending at exorbitant rates, or lending at any interest rate at all.

The condemnation of moneylenders in these societies was offset by the inevitable need for their services. The Roman Republic eventually permitted lending, as did the ancient Greeks and Babylonians. Jewish law was interpreted to allow lending through partnerships called *heter iska*, and the Christian church quietly stopped outright condemnation of the practice of lending at interest in the early 1600s.

The same goes for Linda and me when we're borrowing money to fund Jolliwhip. Or for anyone borrowing to buy a house or a car. Whether we get the money from a bank or the bond market, we still have to pay a certain amount on a certain date, right up until the loan or the bond matures. It makes no difference to us if the person holding our bond or loan decides to sell it to someone else (yes, one can sell loans in the secondary market, just like bonds).

But just because we don't care who buys our debt doesn't mean we shouldn't care where the debt comes from in the first place. Whether you're a consumer or a business, deciding whom to borrow from is very important. For instance, if Linda's car is stolen, and she needs to borrow money to buy a new one, she has a dizzying variety of options from which to choose: She can approach her friends or family—that's a quick option, and could even enjoy a zero interest rate. However, borrowing from friends and family can be risky to our relationships! She could approach a bank or credit union. That would take some time, be moderately expensive and highly restrictive, but there is no relationship risk. She could deploy her credit card. That's a fast way to do things, and is relationship risk–free, but credit cards are expensive and dangerously easy to use. She could go to a payday lender—one of those places that give you a short-term loan until your next paycheck comes in. That's quick money, and relationship risk–free, but payday loans are exorbitant. Finally, she could tap the local loan shark. That's quick money, too, but it's probably even more expensive than a payday loan, and has the added downside of being potentially injurious to her limbs.

The choice of lender is equally important for businesses. A bank can be the best option for someone wanting to move quickly. If Linda and I know the loan officer well, we might even be able to walk out of the bank with a loan on the same day. But the bank will want to insure itself against the possibility of Jolliwhip running into trouble and being unable to pay interest on our loan. The bank might make us pledge **collateral**, or **security**. Maybe we'd offer the bank Linda's holiday home in Palm Springs as collateral, so that if we failed to make our payments or pay the loan back, the bank would take the property instead.

We could go to the bond market for our loan. On the surface, bond investors appear a lot less demanding; they often lend money without asking for any kind of collateral or other restrictions. No security, in other words, which is why bonds are referred to as **unsecured** debt. So it's often easier to get money from the bond market than from a bank, and there are fewer ties. But there are a couple of wrinkles. To compensate for the lack of security, the investors would demand a higher interest payment. And then there's the time factor: putting together a bond deal with investors from all over the country doesn't happen quickly. Getting them to agree on the terms of the **bond deal** can take weeks or even months.

"The better protected you are, the less you have to pay."

Whether they're loans or bonds, so-called **debt instruments** are rarely simple to arrange, and they get more and more complicated the bigger the amount a company needs to borrow. Perhaps the most complex are those loans that investors use to buy companies in a so-called **leveraged buyout**. LBOs, as they're known in the trade, are in essence the purchase of a company using debt, or **leverage**. The investor in an LBO can be a private company or an individual, or even a group of investors. Because they're private entities, and because their investment will buy them a share of the company they're acquiring, the investors' money is called **private equity.**

An LBO looks pretty simple on the face of it. It's really just the way a bunch of people get together and flip a company for a profit.

It's rather like an episode of *Flip This House*, where a family of ten people clubs together to renovate a $10 million mansion in Malibu. Each member of the family chips in $100,000, so they have a down payment of $1 million. Now they go to the bank and borrow $9 million. They buy the mansion, sell off half the land around it, knock down the servants' quarters, and sack everyone but the butler. Then they rewire the place and replace the plumbing. They put in wooden floors, granite countertops, and a steel fridge and two years later, they sell the property for $20 million. The bank gets its money back, and the family divides the $10 million (less interest) that's left. In the end, they each turned $100,000 into nearly $1 million. Not bad in two years!

WHAT'S IN A NAME? ➤

In the leveraged buyout heyday of the 1980s, the people who did these deals were known as buyout shops, or simply as LBO investors.

But a number of high-profile scandals gave the LBO business a bit of a bad rap (and several movies of the period, such as *Wall Street* and *American Psycho*, didn't help much, either). People began calling LBO investors disparaging names. Barbarians at the Gate was one. Asset-strippers was another.

So LBO investors gave themselves a makeover. Today they refer to themselves as **private equity** funds, or **sponsors**.

But they still do exactly the same thing.

Private equity funds do the same thing with companies; they flip them, using the leveraged buyout technique. They get a bunch of investors together to pony up some cash—that's the equity; then they go to the bank and borrow several times that initial amount—that's the leverage; and then they acquire a target company—that's the buyout. They then tweak the company with the aim of making it more profitable, so that they can sell it off in a few years for a profit. Pay back the loan and split the profits. It's a bit like management consultancy on steroids.

The private equity share of the cost of an LBO can be quite low. The key to the success of the transaction is the leverage. It's a bit like a race car driver who's stuck in a rut. She needs to get some wood or stones or straw under the wheel to give it traction and get it moving, but how to get the wheel up in the air first? Leverage! She wedges a plank as far under the wheel as she can, places a fulcrum under it, and by heaving on the end of the plank, she can jack the wheel up. Private equity money is just like that plank. There's usually not very much of it, relative to the size of the company, but if it's used correctly, it can transfer ownership in a billion-dollar enterprise. Of course, private equity money, like the plank, can't do anything on its own. It needs a partner, someone who can apply serious financial pressure to the problem. Someone with lots of money. Like a bank.

Convincing a bank to play ball isn't easy, however. It's hard enough to get *any* kind of loan out of a bank, so getting one to lend you tens of millions of dollars to buy, say, an ice cream company, is a Herculean task. The vast amounts of debt involved in LBO transactions makes them tremendously risky. Once the **target company** is acquired, the sponsors will transfer all the debt to the company's balance sheet. The sponsors then run the company, which has to produce enough revenue to make the interest payments until the loan can be paid down. That's quite a gamble.

Private equity investors pitching an LBO need a good track record, good relationships, and a compelling vision to get a bank on board. Topping the list of a bank's concerns is that the company will **default**, either by missing an interest payment or failing to pay back the money it owes.

So a bank's priorities are, first, to reduce the risk that those two things will happen, and second, to protect itself in the event that they do.

The best way for a bank to manage the risk of default is to put **covenants** in the loan agreement. Covenants are rules that require borrowers to hit certain targets. Perhaps the company has to generate a certain amount of revenue each month, or pay down a certain amount of debt. If the company fails to hit those targets, the bank takes over.

"Thou shalt pay all interest on the fifteenth of the month!"

Other than using covenants, the bank might reduce its risk of the company defaulting by demanding collateral, or simply by charging more money. It might hit the borrower with a big **up-front fee** just to get the loan in the first place. It could levy a **prepayment penalty** in the event a borrower pays a loan off early. Or it could simply charge more interest each month.

The banks that fund LBO deals often demand collateral, covenants, *and* high interest payments, but even with those protections in place, LBOs are often too much for a single bank to handle. For one thing, a single investment of hundreds of millions of dollars is a big bet. And who wants to be the only guy doing the ice cream company deal? Better to have a bunch of other people involved, just for peace of mind. Which is why in many buyouts, the money comes not from one lender, but from a **syndicate**.

Syndicated loans offer some big benefits. On the one hand, lenders don't like being the only person lending money to these big buyouts, or any other big, risky loan, for that matter. But they don't like to be left out of a potential money-making opportunity, either! When a loan is syndicated, it's chopped up into little bits, which allows lenders to pick and choose, and take a little bit of every loan out there. That helps the lenders spread their risk around. Being the only investor in a billion-dollar deal is a bit like going to a cocktail party with an hors d'oeuvres buffet and eating the entire bowl of spinach dip. For one thing, it's risky, since if the loan goes bad because the borrower goes bankrupt, then you lose the entire billion. Moreover, it means you've got less money to spend on other tasty opportunities. Most investors prefer to **diversify** their investments, with a little scoop of this and a forkful of that.

Diversification helps the borrower, too. When lenders are investing in a range of deals, discussion inevitably ensues about who's putting how much money into what, and why. That can create a buzz around the deal. If a portfolio manager tells a friend at another fund that she's investing $5 million in the Jolliwhip deal, the friend might decide it's worth doing the same. Then he tells a few friends of his own, and maybe they buy some, too. It's a bit like chatter at a cocktail party: word gets around, and pretty soon, everyone on the Street is asking for a slice. Or a scoop!

Syndicated loans really caught on in the late 1990s, when investment banks realized they were an alternative to the bond market. Because the loans are sliced into little $5 million pieces, they effectively become **securities**, and they can be traded in a secondary market, just like bonds. Lenders were able to move in and out of certain investments at will and as demand for the syndicated loan product grew, investment banks began arranging loans for all sorts of companies. A restaurant chain wishing to do something risky, like buy out a competitor or expand into China, might have found it tough in the past to get a bank to lend it all the money—those kinds of big projects were far too risky for a single lender to get involved in. But a syndicate of banks? Well, they were

able to spread the risk around. Suddenly companies found themselves able to borrow money to fulfill their wildest business dreams. PepsiCo, for example, borrowed $10 billion to spin off the KFC, Taco Bell, and Pizza Hut fast-food chains in 1997. And the communications company Global Crossing convinced investors to give them a total of $12 billion to string a network of telecommunication cables under the seas.

Whether it's used to buy a carmaker or an ice cream company, a corporate loan will likely come with what's called a variable or **floating rate** of interest. This is very different from a consumer loan, such as the 30-year mortgage, which will usually come with a **fixed rate** of interest. A fixed rate means the borrower will pay the same amount every payment period until the loan matures. The interest on a floating-rate loan, on the other hand, can adjust from month to month.

One way to think of a floating-rate loan is to picture a sailor in the crow's nest of a ship, fifty feet above the surface of the sea. The ship is anchored in a bay with a tide that varies widely from day to day. The sailor's height from the seafloor rises and falls as the tide goes in and out; at noon, he's just fifty-five feet above the seafloor, but at five p.m. he's eighty feet up—yet his height above the water is always just fifty feet. But his height above the water level is a constant fifty feet throughout.

A floating-rate loan has two parts: the **base rate**, which moves up and down, just like the sea level; and the **spread** or **margin**, which is a fixed amount above the base rate. In our sailor's case the fixed amount is a distance of fifty feet; in a loan it's a fixed percentage. The base rate is often the percentage that banks charge their best companies, called the **prime rate**, or often simply "Prime." Prime goes up and down, just like the tide, depending on the state of the economy and other factors. Because of this, if you borrow a fixed-rate loan that's 3 percent over Prime, and Prime goes to 5 percent, you'll have to pay 8 percent. But if Prime falls to 1 percent, you're only paying 4 percent.

FLOATING RATE VS. ADJUSTABLE RATE ➤

A lot of people who bought houses in the boom of the 2000s did so with the help of an adjustable-rate mortgage, or ARM. An ARM is similar to a floating-rate loan, in that the interest on both will change as their base rates move up and down.

But while the interest rate on a floating-rate loan changes all the time, an ARM's interest rate adjusts much less frequently.

Many ARMs are hybrids, with an initial fixed interest rate for a certain period that converts to an adjustable rate later in the life of the loan.

ARMs got a bad reputation during the 2008 financial crisis when it became clear that many borrowers were lured by an initial low rate of interest, but were unable to make the higher payments when the adjustment eventually kicked in.

While Linda and I shop for a loan for Jolliwhip, it occurs to us that deciding between a floating rate and a fixed rate is a bit like making a wager. We discover that bondholders are demanding 8 percent interest—that's a fixed rate that we'd have to pay every year. Prime is just 1 percent, and the bank wants us to pay Prime plus 6 percent—7 percent in total, at first. So we'd get a better deal from the bank initially.

But then we hear on the radio that interest rates are likely to rise significantly over the next two years. In our case, they only have to rise 2 percent before we'll be paying more than we would if we went with the bond market. Do we go for the certainty of a fixed payment or do we take a risk in the hopes of paying less over time? Decisions, decisions!

Unfortunately, we do have to make a decision if we are to grow our ice cream business in the way we envision. Do we sell a piece of the company or do we borrow? Do we use bonds or a bank loan? Secured or unsecured? Fixed or floating?

All of our choices matter, and not just because of the cost and the hassle: the kind of financing a company chooses can change the way it appears to investors, and even change the way it does business. In this way, a company is a bit like a cookie. As anyone who makes cookies at home knows, you can change everything about a cookie by adjusting the ingredients. More flour makes the cookie look like a scone; more butter and it spreads out flat. In a company's case, the core ingredients are its equity and its debt. Depending on the amount of equity or debt that a company has on its books, it will look very different to an accountant or a regulator.

This financial composition of a company is called **capital structure**. In the next chapter we'll learn how capital structure can govern everything about a company, from how it attracts money from investors to the way it goes about its daily business.

CHAPTER THREE

Under the Skin

How a Company Hangs Together

Ask most people what makes a company, and they'll probably talk about the kind of business it does, the products it makes, where it's located, the people who work for it, and maybe even the buildings that house it.

Investors look at all these things, too, but what's often most important to them is hidden under the surface. They're a bit like doctors who know that, just because people look great on the outside, it doesn't necessarily mean they're healthy.

When I visit my doctor, she always makes a big deal about my diet. She asks what I eat, what I drink, how much red meat, how many veggies, how much alcohol, and so on. It's key to her understanding of my state of health and my body's function. It may even be key to her understanding of my body's composition: if I stuff myself with junk food every day, I might end up with too much belly fat. A preponderance of eggs and shrimp, and I could ratchet up my cholesterol—you are what you eat, after all.

It's the same for companies: *they are what they eat*. And all companies eat cash. Lots of it. The cash goes to pay staff, buy raw materials, replace old furniture, acquire new technology, pay rent. To operate, in other words. You need money to make money, as they say. But investors want to know where that money comes from. How much comes from sales? How much from lenders? How much from equity investors? The answer can make a company look very different from the way it appears in the news, or in its glossy annual report. And it can make all the difference to an investor who's trying to decide whether she wants to lend to the company, buy shares, or invest in some other way.

In a company, as in any kind of structure, there's stuff on the top of the pile, stuff at the bottom, and other stuff in the middle. In this example, the stuff is the investors, and they're arranged by **seniority**, with people who've made bank loans to the company at the top, bondholders in the middle, and shareholders at the bottom.

A good way of thinking about capital structure is to picture a passenger airplane. Most aircraft are divided by class: first class, business, economy. Companies are exactly the same. Up in the nose, in those sumptuous first-class recliners, sit the bankers. They've made big loans to the company. Next up, in the not-quite-so-plush-but-still-very-comfortable seats, sit the business-class passengers—the bondholders. And finally, crammed into the back, nine abreast with just seventeen inches of leg-room, are the economy passengers—the shareholders.

All the passengers have paid cash for their seats. The cash pays for the fuel, which gets them off the ground and into the air, and up to a cruising altitude of 30,000 feet. For a while the plane flies smoothly. But after a few hours, while it's above the ocean, things start to go awry. The weather is unexpectedly bad and the pilot is forced to make a long detour. Before long, the plane is over land, but it's a long way from its destination and the fuel is beginning to run low. As the fuel warning light flickers on, the pilot decides to make an emergency landing at a small airstrip.

The plane lands safely, and no one is hurt. But when it comes to evacuating the plane, who gets looked after first? First class, of course! They're whisked away in comfortable limousines. Then a luxury coach pulls up and the business class passengers climb aboard. Now it's time for

those in economy to be shuttled away. The airline has requested a fleet of local buses, but they're late. They broke down, so passengers are forced to walk.

The same thing happens in a company. Investors pay money into the firm, and depending on what kind of investment they make, they are seated higher or lower in the seniority stakes. The money the investors have put into the company is used to run the company's operations, and all's well when there's plenty of money to spend. But once the company runs low on cash, it has to start thinking about how to deal with its investors.

Why? Because when a company's in trouble, investors want out. And they want their money back. But trouble usually means that a company doesn't have enough money to operate, which also means it doesn't have the money it needs to repay its investors in full, either. Fortunately for the company, it doesn't have to decide who to pay first; the capital structure makes that process easy.

The loan investors get their money back before anyone else, because their debt is the safest and the cheapest: they demanded collateral from the company, and probably had some covenants in the agreement, too, so that if the company slipped up at any point, they'd get an early warning. If the company can't give these lenders all their money, the lenders will take the collateral, whether it's in the form of equipment, real estate, or even whole divisions of the company. If there's cash left over after the senior lenders are paid, the bondholders will get their money back. And after the bondholders are repaid, if there's any cash in the bank, the shareholders get their investment principal back, although, if a company is in real trouble, they're often left with nothing.

Place Your Bets! How Risk Factors In

The capital structure of a company is all about risk and reward: the more an investor risks, the bigger the reward (that is, if things go well). Anyone who has ever tried to negotiate a bank loan knows that banks hate risk. It's their job to lend money, but they will always do their best to reduce their risk as much as possible. To do this, they add covenants into the agreement and ask for collateral to secure the loan. In return for this considerable security and the lower risk that results, they're prepared to take less reward in the form of a smaller interest payment. In short, the knowledge that he's highly likely to get his money back is worth more to the banker than a fat monthly check.

Bondholders want a bit more of a reward, so they're willing to take a bit more risk. In fact, they're prepared to let the banks get paid first if something goes wrong, knowing that could mean the bondholders might not get their money back at all. But in exchange for taking that risk, bondholders invariably ask for, and deserve, a bigger reward, in the form of a higher interest rate. They also get the added security of knowing they're not last in line to get paid if the company runs into trouble.

That honor goes to the company's shareholders. When companies go bankrupt, it's not uncommon to read stories about shareholders ending up with nothing, or being **wiped out**. Being last in line isn't much fun when things go wrong in a company, but when the company's performing well, shareholders do better than anyone. That's because, unlike bonds or bank debt, shares can soar in price, many times over, and the chance of reward, or **upside**, is enormous. In fact, there's really no limit to the price to which a share can rise, and shareholders can make their money many times over if they buy low and sell high. Lenders, on the other hand, get paid only a fixed rate of interest on their investments.

SHELL GAME ➤

Some companies appear quite respectable and conventional at a glance, but open them up and they're empty inside. No staff, no assets, no operations, nothing.

These so-called shell companies can be legal, but they're often used for nefarious purposes, such as dodging taxes, or, in the case of Enron, hiding losses made by another company.

There's often no way to tell if a company is a shell without cracking it open, although the names of Enron's shell companies were a bit of a giveaway: JEDI, Chewco, Kenobe, and Obi-1, all inspired by characters from the movie *Star Wars*.

You can see why investors are so interested in studying the company's capital structure. If our ice cream company decides to issue bonds, potential bondholders will want to see who the other investors are in the company's hierarchy. They probably won't care if we've sold all the shares in my company to the public (they'll be ahead of the shareholders, after all), but if we've borrowed an enormous loan from a bunch of banks who'll be ahead of them in the capital structure, they might not be so keen to invest. Alternatively, they could insist on a hefty interest rate to compensate for the risk they're taking by being second in line if things go wrong. A smart stock investor thinking about buying shares in our company might also balk if she sees we have a lot of debt—a little math might reveal that if things go wrong for our company, there wouldn't be anything left for shareholders.

Once all of these investors have given us their money and taken up position in our capital structure, the company's finances appear nice and orderly. The capital structure shows the company accountants and other potential investors how much debt there is and where it's located, how much equity the company has outstanding, and how much ready cash the company has to spend. It also illustrates which investors are senior and who will be last in line if things go wrong. But when bad stuff happens in a company, investors don't always follow the playbook to the letter. You can imagine the chaos in an aircraft if something went wrong and the plane had to crash-land—everyone would be fighting for the exit. The same thing usually happens in a troubled corporation. Anyone with a stake is suddenly scrambling to get a piece of the action, and lawsuits fly as shareholders and bondholders battle with the banks for a share of whatever money there is left in the company. A company in this situation will often end up in court, where a judge will decide who gets what, or at least she'll try to persuade the various groups of investors to agree.

And once a company ends up in court, it's treated in a similar way to a downed aircraft that's been hauled into a special hangar for an examination. The company is stripped down and cut open, and crews of accountants and attorneys crawl into every nook and cranny, trying to determine what brought it down and what bits they can save.

The company's **balance sheet** usually offers some significant clues. The balance sheet is a snapshot of the company's finances and therefore its capital structure. It reveals how much money comes in and goes out of the company in a given period. It shows you how much cash the company has, a result of the goods and the shares that it has sold, and, most important, how much money the company owes.

In almost all bankruptcy cases, the gunk clogging up the engine is debt. To be bankrupt means to be unable to pay back what one owes. It doesn't mean a company can't make money: it means a company can't make *enough* money. A company could make a billion dollars a year, but if it can't pay the interest on its loans, or pay back the money it has borrowed, it's bankrupt.

Debt can be equally deadly to a big company or a small one, if it's not handled properly. It doesn't matter how little a company borrows,

either. Our tiny ice cream company might borrow just $2 million to buy that new property, hoping to pay the money back in two years. But what happens if the economy goes sour? Or the price of milk triples? Or, more simply, just not enough people like our ice cream? These are problems, to be sure, but the real issue remains that crushing load of debt, the big monthly payments, and the fact we'd have to find *two million dollars* somewhere in two years' time.

Bankruptcies are all about debt, but they often look as though they're about something else. When Enron failed in 2001, people pointed the finger at its creative accounting practices. When Global Crossing was sunk in 2002, people blamed the company's extravagant spending. When General Motors and Chrysler went bankrupt in 2009, people blamed everything from the companies' legacy payments to their poorly made cars. In each case, it wasn't so much the companies' strategies that bled them dry as it was the billions of dollars they had borrowed to put their strategies into action.

In other words, these companies were all strangled to death by a single murderer: debt. Even in the case of Lehman Brothers, which at $691 billion will go down in history as one of the biggest bankruptcies ever, it was debt that pulled the company under. But when people talk about Lehman Brothers, they rarely talk about the company's debt—instead they often refer to the investments that it and many other companies made in the boom years of 2003 to 2007. These investments can be so complicated that they make bonds and shares look like children's toys compared to a jet engine. Just mentioning them can make seasoned financiers twitch and shiver. These investments have been called everything from "the devil's own instruments" to "financial weapons of mass destruction."

I call them by their real name . . .

Derivatives.

CHAPTER FOUR

Derivatives

Devilish? Destructive? Deadly?

It's true, derivatives do have a terrible reputation. Who doesn't grit their teeth at the mention of a CDO, or roll their eyes when people start talking about futures and options? Derivatives have gotten us into trouble so many times that it's no wonder they're regarded by many people as the serial killers of the financial markets. We know that they brought down Lehman Brothers in 2008, but it wasn't just Lehman. Bear Stearns, AIG, IndyMac, and Washington Mutual were all punctured by derivatives to some extent. What torpedoed Barings Bank back in 1995? Derivatives. What skewered Long-Term Capital Management in 1998? Derivatives. What scuppered the South Sea Company all the way back in 1720? You guessed it. The list of victims of derivatives is long and bloody.

One reason derivatives are so deadly is that they can become extremely complicated. A diagram of a collateralized debt obligation, or CDO, for example, looks a bit like the representation of the structure of a fuel molecule, or the working of a spaceship: designed by rocket scientists and decipherable only by experts.

While it's true that many derivatives are devilishly complex, it's also true that most derivatives are dead simple. So simple, in fact, that we use them every day.

The word *derivative* means something that's *derived* from something else. Gasoline, for example, is derived from oil, and the price of a gallon of gas is related to the cost of a barrel of oil. If oil prices rise, gas prices likely will, too. The same goes for oranges and orange juice: if the orange harvest is small, oranges become more expensive. Orange juice is derived from oranges, so OJ prices will likely rise as well.

Orange juice and gasoline are not derivatives in the financial sense. But understanding the relationship between the cost of a raw material and its by-product can help explain the basics of a financial derivative. Because a financial derivative also consists of two related parts: the underlying asset and the derivative itself.

The underlying asset may be a thousand barrels of oil, or it may be a car loan. The derivative is simply a contract based on an asset.

Okay, maybe that's not so simple. So here's an example using . . . turkeys!

Every year, in the month before Thanksgiving, stores all over America offer people the chance to reserve their turkeys in advance. I've been doing this for years, ever since 2000, when I left this task until the last minute—Thanksgiving eve—and found that all the stores in my New York neighborhood had sold out. I eventually found my turkey: it was a tiny, misshapen, half-frozen thing that I bought from a bodega. It cost me a small fortune, and it tasted awful.

Never again.

So like so many Americans, I now reserve my turkey. I go into the store as soon as they start advertising the service, and request a twenty-six-pounder that I can pick up two days before the holiday. The clerk tells me my turkey will cost $25. He takes an impression of my credit card, just in case I fail to show up or pay up, and he gives me a signed, dated claim check, which says something like "The holder of this claim check has agreed to buy one 26 lb. turkey, for the price of $25, on or before November 27 of this year."

That claim check is a derivative contract, known as a **future**, and it works the same way, whether the underlying asset is a turkey or a thousand barrels of light sweet crude oil. The price I agree to pay is called the **strike price**, and the date of pickup is called the **delivery date**.

Regular people may not use these technical terms, but we do use this kind of basic contract all the time to reserve goods and services. We do it just in case—in case the store runs out; in case the rental company runs out of cars; or in case the airline sells all the seats on the flight we want to take. Service providers like to use these contracts, too. Knowing in advance how many people want turkeys for Thanksgiving helps my local store owner ensure his shelves are stocked efficiently. This knowledge also helps him buy birds in bulk at a discount and make some extra money on the deal.

There are downsides to futures. For one thing, they're not very flexible. A future is an agreement to take or make delivery on a certain date, at a certain price. The store has my credit card details, remember. And that inflexibility might present some problems for me. For example, what if my mother-in-law turns up the weekend before the Thanksgiving holiday with a goose? Suddenly I'm in danger of being charged $25 for a turkey that I don't need and won't use.

I could freeze the turkey. But there is an alternative: I could sell my claim check to someone else, or as they say in the financial world, I could **trade** that future.

To do so, I pop next door to speak to my neighbor. It turns out she needs a bird this year and she's happy to pay $25. The trade is on!

I give her my claim check. Now, she can either pay for the turkey herself when she uses that claim check, or she can pay me $25 cash at this point and the store will just charge my credit card when she picks up the bird. I don't care so long as I'm not out $25. The storekeeper doesn't care who pays—so long as someone does.

And that's how futures contracts are traded. The contracts are formalized so that the trades can take place on exchanges, but they're really as simple as that.

Futures are great for people who are sure they want to buy something at some point in the future. But what if you're not sure? One of the reasons I was so late buying that turkey in New York in 2000 was that I didn't know until the last minute whether I would need a turkey or not. Members of my family have a habit of turning up at my house laden with food, and without telling me beforehand. And sometimes they show up empty-handed, which means I have to go shopping. Because of this, I need to be able to reserve a turkey for Thanksgiving but without a commitment to buy it.

In other words, I want the **option** of buying a turkey.

Back at the store, the owner tells me if I buy a twenty-six-pound turkey today, it'll cost me $25—that's what called the **spot price**. He's happy to reserve a bird for me at that price, but only if I pay a deposit of $5, which I'll forfeit if I don't actually buy the goods by Thanksgiving Day. Once again I get a signed, dated claim check, but this one is worded a bit differently: "This check gives the holder the *right* to buy one 26 lb. turkey for the price of $25, before November 27 of this year."

In Wall Street jargon, my claim check is a **call**. It's a kind of option that gives me the right, but not the obligation, to buy something. I don't have to pick that turkey up. If I don't, however, the option will **expire** and I'll forfeit my five bucks. But if I do want it, it'll be there for me, guaranteed, at a total cost of $30 ($25 turkey plus $5 option).

A week later, I see this story in the paper.

TURKEY PRICES SOAR AS BIRDS FLY THE COOP

Modesto, Calif. 23 November—AP

—Turkey farmers in California are reporting that the normally flightless birds are taking to the air. Hundreds of thousands of birds, perhaps 70 percent of all California turkeys, have escaped from farms all over the state, simply by flying out of their cages, a spokesman from the California Turkey Cooperative said today. He said because turkeys do not fly, they are generally kept in roofless pens, so those birds that have learned how to fly were therefore able to escape quite easily.

Reports from the U.S. Department of Agriculture and the Meteorological Survey suggest that the birds have flown south— maybe just for the winter; or maybe forever.

Just as the turkeys have taken off, so have turkey prices. The average price of a 20-pound California-grown turkey hen is now up to $100 and climbing, a spokeswoman for the American Poultry Association said. Supermarket poultry aisles are emptying out as shoppers rush to grab a turkey ahead of the Thanksgiving holiday.

Now, most people might read this story and marvel that turkeys have somehow magically regained the power of flight. I'm more excited by the news that turkeys are now selling for $100! And I have a claim check that guarantees me a bird at $25! I'm feeling pretty smart right now: if my relatives show up empty-handed for the holiday, I can buy a turkey at nearly a quarter of the going price. And if they arrive laden with all sorts of delicious foods and I don't need to buy a turkey, I'm only out five bucks.

Or am I?

A week before the holiday, my mother-in-law arrives with not one, but *two* turkeys! Clearly I'm not going to use my claim check, or **exercise** my option, as financial people call this transaction. Pity about that five bucks, I think, and then I remember the trick I pulled off last year: I was able to sell my claim check to my neighbor. Maybe she needs a turkey again this year?

No. She did the smart thing and reserved her own bird. But she's glad I called, because Cyril, her boss, has been panicking about having twenty people coming to dinner—and he hasn't bought a turkey yet.

Maybe Cyril would like to buy my option?

I could charge him just $5. Then I'd be even, and he would end up paying a total of just $30 for the bird. A bargain for him, under the circumstances.

Or I could make a little money on the deal.

I arrange to meet Cyril in a coffee shop. I ask him how much he's prepared to pay for a twenty-six-pound turkey. He tells me he'll pay up to $50, but no more: he'd rather eat meat loaf than fork out more than fifty bucks for a bird.

I nod sympathetically and tell him I have a way for him to get a turkey for exactly that price. By paying me $25 for my claim check, then exercising the option and paying the store $25, he'll get a twenty-six-pound turkey for $50.

CYRIL'S CHOICE	
Either	
Buy a turkey today from the store (spot price)	$100
Or	
Buy (a) my claim check (option)	$25
Plus	
(b) my reserved turkey (strike price)	$25
Total (a +b)	$50

Nice trade! By selling my option for $25, I make $20 (I had to pay that $5 deposit to buy the option, remember). That's an 80 percent profit! And Cyril wins, too. He gets to brag to his guests about how he managed to buy a hormone-free, free-range turkey for *half* the going price.

My turkey option was a call, an option to buy something. Options aren't just about buying stuff, however. You can use options to reserve the right to sell things, too. In the financial world, an option to sell is called a **put**.

If you've ever sold a car online, you'll know that used-car dealers often call up and offer you a price for your vehicle. A put allows you to lock in that sale price. For a fee. Here's how a conversation to arrange a put option might go:

> **DEALER:** Hi, I'm calling from WildWheels Auto, out on Midden Road. We saw you're selling your 2004 Volvo, and we're prepared to offer you $10,000 for it.
>
> **ME:** That's not a bad price, but I'd like to shop around a bit more. Is there any way I can buy an option to sell this car to you?
>
> **DEALER:** How would that work?
>
> **ME:** Well, I'll pay you $500 in cash via Paypal, right now, for the right to sell you my Volvo for $10,000 by close of business Friday. If I don't show up by then, you keep the $500. If I do show up, then you pay me $10,000 for my ride.
>
> **DEALER:** What about the $500?
>
> **ME:** You get to keep that. It's your fee.
>
> **DEALER:** You've got a deal.

With this agreement, I have locked in a price of $10,000 for my car, until close of business Friday. That gives me a week to shop the car around for a better deal. If I can find someone willing to pay more than

$10,500 for the Volvo, then I'll sell the car to that person. The agreement with WildWheels Auto will expire on Friday afternoon and the dealer will keep my $500.

But what if I can't find anyone who wants to buy a used Volvo—or anyone willing to pay more than nine grand for my sweet ride? It's a good thing I locked in that price with WildWheels.

All week long, people call about the car, but no one wants to pay me more than $8,000. So on Friday afternoon I decide to **exercise my option**. I drive my car onto the WildWheels lot, and the dealer gives me a check for $10,000. Of course, he keeps his fee, which means I net just $9,500, but it's worth it—I'm still getting $500 more than if I sold the car to one of my alternate buyers.

When we hear talk about futures and options in the financial world, it's often in connection with **commodities**. A commodity is something that costs the same wherever it is produced. An ounce of gold that's dug out of a mine in the Philippines, for example, costs the same as an ounce of gold panned out of a stream in Alaska. The same goes for corn, wheat, steel, copper, and a whole host of other products. It also goes for less traditional commodities, such as currencies, securities, and even interest rates.

People buy and sell commodities all the time, but most of the activity in the futures and options markets takes place on trading desks in office towers, far away from the fields and mines where commodities are produced, or the wharves and stockyards where the goods actually change hands.

The futures and options markets allow bankers and investors to profit from movements in the markets of commodities without actually having to own the product.

Let's return to the turkey example. Things are now back to normal and turkeys are once again flightless. Still, my neighbor Clara and I have been watching the price of turkeys soar over the last week. Because feed prices are rising, farmers are passing on the cost to consumers. A twenty-six-pound bird now costs $50! Clara is convinced the price will go even higher, but I think people would rather eat tofurkey than pay ridiculous amounts for a flightless bird. Clara proposes a wager.

> **CLARA:** I want you to sell me a turkey future.
>
> **ME:** But I don't have a turkey, Clara!
>
> **CLARA:** You don't need one. All you need is a blank check.
>
> **ME:** I'm not giving you a blank check!
>
> **CLARA:** No, silly. You're going to keep it—for now. Just make it out to me and sign it, then leave the dollar amount blank. Then put the check in an envelope, write "Turkey" on the front, and slip it in your desk drawer.
>
> **ME:** Okay. Weird. What next?
>
> **CLARA:** Next you write me a claim. Something like "This claim gives the bearer the right to receive the value of one twenty-six-pound turkey in return for the amount of fifty bucks, delivery and payment to be made at eight a.m. on Thanksgiving Day."

ME: Okay, but I still don't get it.

CLARA: Here's the thing. At eight a.m. on Thanksgiving Day, I'm going to give you a fifty-dollar bill, and you're gonna give me a turkey.

ME: But I don't have a turkey.

CLARA: I know, silly. So you're going to give me the cash equivalent. You're going to open the envelope, call the store, and ask how much a twenty-six-pound turkey costs. Whatever number the clerk gives you, you write down on the check. Then you give the check to me.

ME: Aha! Now I get it!

It's a tense few days as we approach Thanksgiving. I dream each night about Clara coming by at 8 a.m., handing me the $50, and watching as I open up the envelope.

In my dream, I call the store, speak to the clerk, and then write the number that he gives me on the check. Clara hands me $50, and I hand her the check.

Boy, is she happy. Turkeys are $100! She has given me a $50 bill, but I've handed her a $100 check! She's made $50!

The next night I dream again. There's her $50. There's the check. The phone call. The clerk. The number. She's not so happy now. A turkey costs just $20, so I've given her a $20 check, but she's given me $50. This time, I'm the winner: I've made $30 on the deal.

We're geniuses! We've managed to find a way to make a bet on the turkey market without even having to look at a turkey—let alone deliver one.

Except we're not really geniuses. The financial folks who trade futures take part in these kinds of transactions all the time. Instead of taking delivery of a physical commodity, they use what's called **cash settlement**. You can do this with put options and call options as well: all you have to do is find someone who'll take the bet.

That's right—the bet, the wager, the gamble. No wonder people think Wall Street is a casino—there are plenty of similarities, especially when it comes to derivatives: someone who's buying oil futures may be betting that unrest in the Middle East will choke off supply and spike prices; someone selling an orange juice call option may suspect a warm growing season led to a bumper crop; someone buying gold puts may be banking on an improving global economy and a drop in demand for the precious metal. Uncertainty can make money if you're on the right side of the trade. Certainty can make money, too. It's the desire for certainty that makes the actual producers and buyers of commodities invest in futures and options in the first place. And it's the desire for certainty that gave birth to one of the least understood, yet most common, derivatives in the market today—the **swap**.

CHAPTER FIVE

Your Jell-O for My Cake

How Swaps Work

f derivatives have a bad name, swaps have a *really* bad name. One type of swap, the credit default swap, was referred to as a financial weapon of mass destruction by the famous investor Warren Buffett. Swaps are derivatives, just like futures and options, but they look so different from their cousins that they're often handled separately by the banks and investment companies that deal in them.

How can that be? Most people already know what the word *swap* means. Most of us start swapping stuff at school: a loan of my jump rope for a go on your video game; your cool scarf for my cute bracelet. And food—kids are always swapping food, whether it's the food they bring in packed lunches, or the stuff they get served in the cafeteria.

I once visited a school where the kids bought set meal plans. Plan A was vegetarian, and Plan B was for kids who could eat meat. Both had lots of variety for the main courses and the drinks, but while the desserts on Plan B were different each day, the kids on Plan A always had Jell-O.

	PLAN A	PLAN B
Main	Vegetarian (varied)	Nonvegetarian (varied)
Drink	Soda or milk (varied)	Soda or milk (varied)
Dessert	Jell-O (always)	Cake, ice cream (varied)

I asked about this—were the Plan B desserts nonvegetarian? Apparently not: it was just the way the caterer had designed the meal plans. Wow, I thought. Sucks to be on Plan A. Jell-O every day? Boring!

But this, of course, is where a swap comes in. A child who's vegetarian and who doesn't want to eat Jell-O every day can always try to find someone to take her Jell-O in return for a slice of cake on the days she doesn't fancy her assigned dessert. Fair enough. But what if she really, really hates Jell-O? And what if finding a swap partner every day is time-consuming and uncertain?

What she really wants is the Plan B dessert: a little variety and, more importantly, no Jell-O. Which means she needs to find someone on Plan B who loves Jell-O. Someone who loves Jell-O so much, they want to eat it every day.

A simple swap. It's the kind of agreement that happens every day in school lunchrooms all over America. And it happens on financial companies' swap desks all over the world.

Perhaps the simplest swap has to do with the interest rates on loans. Some loans come with a fixed interest rate: my home loan, for example, might have a rate of 5 percent a year over five years. But my neighbor, Clara, might have a loan with a *floating* rate: 3 percent over the prime rate every year over five years.

Clara and I both bought our houses for the same price at the same time. Since then, she has quit her job, and now she's on a tight budget. And a floating-rate loan makes it hard to budget: she never knows what the prime rate will be from one month to the next, which means she is never certain how much she will owe the bank. It could be 4 percent, or it could be 6 percent. So my flat 5 percent loan looks very appealing. As for me, I'm happy to take a gamble. If prime falls, I could pay as little as 3.5 percent, which looks pretty sweet. But I'm stuck with this fixed rate loan. So one day I approach her with a solution—why don't I just pay the interest that she owes each month, and she can pay what I owe. In other words, why don't we swap?

It's the same for companies. Some get fixed rate loans, and others get floating-rate loans. Sometimes they ask for a certain type of loan but then find out it doesn't work for them: it might be too expensive, or their business needs might change, and they don't want to pay a big fee to re-finance. Sometimes businesses don't have a choice, and they might have to take what they can get from the bank.

Say Jolliwhip has a $1 million floating-rate loan. Linda and I got it because it was the lowest rate we could find at the time, but it's not working for us anymore. It's winter, and the ice cream business is in a bit of a slump, and we need to budget very precisely each month. Not knowing what we'll have to pay for our loan isn't helping.

I ask my loan officer, who suggests a visit to an **investment bank** . . .

Inside the offices of the Santa Barbara boutique investment bank Fleessem & Selle, I perch on the edge of an overstuffed faux-antique leather chair, chafing in a business suit. On the other side of an enormous, empty teak desk, Ian the i-banker lounges in a plush executive chair, dressed in artfully rumpled chinos and a golf shirt.

Me: So, I've got this floating-rate loan with JT Gorgon. It's making my life really tough right now: I have to pay 5 percent one month, 6 percent the next, and 4 percent the month after that! It's making it hard to keep my books straight, and I heard you might be able to help.

Ian the i-Banker: Dude, I get it. I can take that uncertainty away.

Me: How?

Ian the i-Banker: By working out a deal for you to pay a fixed interest rate every month. Say five and a half percent. That's $55,000.

Me: Okay, paying 55K every month would be great. But how am I going to convince Gorgon to accept that?

Ian the i-Banker: You don't. You still have to pay Gorgon, but you use our money.

Me: I'm confused.

Ian the i-Banker: Here's how it works. Every month, you get a bill from Gorgon, right?

Me: Yes.

Ian the i-Banker: Okay, from now on, every month, as soon as you get that bill, you call me. I'll write you a check for what you owe Gorgon, and in return, you send me $55,000. Then you just take the money I paid you, and give it to Gorgon.

Me: You're telling me that if I pay you $55K each month, you're going to pay Gorgon.

Ian the i-Banker: Yes, except I'm using you as the go-between. But that's basically right—in return for a fixed

	amount each month, we're agreeing to pay off your loan, no matter how much it costs.
ME:	Okay, but what if my payments to JT Gorgon fall below $55,000 a month?
IAN THE I-BANKER:	In that case, we benefit, because you'll be paying us more than you owe Gorgon. But say interest rates rise, and that bill from Gorgon jumps to 7 percent—that's $70,000 you owe now! Except that you don't owe it: we do. You keep on paying us $55,000 flat, and we pay whatever the loan costs.
ME:	Hmm. I'm tempted . . .

You can see the appeal. I'm on a tight budget, so I want to know exactly how much I'm paying each month. Fleessem & Selle can help me. I might end up paying more overall, but that's the price of certainty. This transaction is called an **interest rate swap**, where I'm exchanging, or swapping, my interest rate with the investment bank.

I'm considering this deal because I want a flat, fixed interest rate that will make it easier for me to manage my budget. But there are other reasons to enter into a swap like this. If I suspect interest rates will rise over the next year or so, I might want to lock in a fixed rate, just in case.

In my conversation with Ian, I got the impression that Fleessem will be taking on the risk (or benefits) of the moves in interest rates. But investment banks and other financial companies that are involved in swaps quite often try to find someone else to take on that risk, instead. In that case, the investment bank is just a go-between, putting someone who wants a fixed rate together with someone who wants a floating rate.

BIG BLUE AND THE WORLD BANK ›

The first interest rate swap took place in 1981, between the computer company IBM and the World Bank.

IBM had borrowed a large sum in deutschmarks, which weakened in value against the U.S. dollar.

The company could have dealt with the problem by borrowing dollars, converting them to deutschmarks, and paying down the deutschmark loan. But that would have doubled its debt load for a while and looked bad on its balance sheet.

Instead IBM swapped its loan obligation with a dollar loan obligation held by the World Bank. The idea caught on quickly, and interest rate swaps are one of the most frequently traded derivatives today.

Another common type of swap involves commodities. The price of a commodity can vary widely: up one day, and down the next. If you're in the kind of business that buys a certain commodity a great deal throughout the year, this can be a problem.

It's a bit like coping with the cost of raw materials for our ice cream company. We have to buy a hundred gallons of fresh cream from Springfield Dairy every week to make our product. But the price of cream can vary dramatically from month to month, and from season to season. Now that we're on a budget, that can cause us as much of a problem as our variable loans caused us. So I wonder to myself—if I can level out my loan costs, can I do the same for my cream expenditure?

I drop in at Fleessem's to see Ian, who tells me that, yes, it is possible. Our last deal allowed me to swap my **interest rate risk** for a fixed payment—this time, he tells me, I'm taking a big **commodities price risk**. One month my bill for four hundred gallons of fresh cream might be $10,000; another month it might be $15,000. Ian tells me his bank is willing to take that risk by letting me swap that variable payment for a fixed payment, say $13,000 each month. If I agree, I will pay the bank a set amount each month, making it easy for me to budget, and the bank will pay whatever the dairy charges: the swap will transfer the risk from me to the bank.

The swap is all about exchanging something unknown—whether it be an uncertain interest rate each month or a surprise dessert for lunch—for something defined, such as a fixed payment each month, or Jell-O every day. Uncertainty is risky, but it can also be rewarding, which is why banks can often find someone to take that risk, or may even be prepared to take part in the swap themselves. The name they have for the people involved on either side of the swap is **counterparty**. The two kids who swap desserts in the lunchroom are counterparties in that deal; in my interest rate swap, my ice cream company is one counterparty and the bank is the other.

Risk comes in all shapes and sizes in the financial world, but there's often someone who's prepared to take on that risk—for a fee. The biggest players in the risk game have traditionally been the insurance companies.

Their business is all about taking on risk, whether it be the risk that one of our drivers might crash my ice cream truck, or you might sink your boat, or a tree might fall down on my house. If any of those things happen, and we don't have insurance, we're on the hook for the full amount. That's an unknown cost that could be very hefty. But in exchange for a small monthly fee, the insurance company will go on the hook for us: it will swap our risk for an income stream. In effect, then, the insurance policies are swaps: a truck-crash swap; a sunken-boat swap; a destroyed-house swap.

The insurance business has been swapping risk for fixed payments for centuries, but it wasn't until the 1980s that Wall Street financiers worked out how they could use the principle to make money themselves. Once they got going, however, they didn't look back: today swaps are some of the most frequently traded contracts in the world.

Thinking about swaps as a kind of insurance is the easiest way to understand the most infamous member of the swap family: the **credit default swap**, or CDS. CDSs were at the very heart of the 2008 financial crisis, and as such were labeled with all sorts of apocalyptic nicknames—Warren Buffett's "financial weapons of mass destruction" line was merely the most publicized dig at them.

The reputation of this swap isn't helped by its name: *credit default swap* just sounds horribly complicated, doesn't it? And then there's that three-letter designation, which lumps the poor CDS in with truly com-

plex products such as ABS, CDO, CLO, and MBS, and scares most normal people stiff.

But the credit default swap isn't that complicated. In essence, it's just insurance. Like the insurance on my ice cream truck: if I don't insure the truck, then I take the risk that I'll have to pay $50,000 for a new vehicle if it's totaled. So I pay the insurance company $100 a month to take that risk for me. That's my truck-crash swap, where I've swapped the risk of the crash for a monthly payment.

In a CDS the risk isn't of a truck crashing or a boat sinking; it's of a credit defaulting. A "credit" is another word for a bond, or a loan, or another kind of debt. And an "event of default" is when someone fails to pay interest on their loan. So a "credit default" means a borrower can't pay interest on his loan.

When Linda and I first started Jolliwhip, we took out a five-year, $500,000 loan to buy equipment and renovate a building. It was a pretty risky loan for the bank to keep on its books, because as soon as we set up shop, frozen yogurt exploded into the local market . . .

LOAN OFFICER: Mr. Houston, we have a problem.

BANK CEO: Problem?

LOAN OFFICER: Yessir. You see, I approved a loan to the Jolliwhip ice cream company a few months ago, but the frozen treats market has changed a bit since then. Have you heard of BuzzBerry?

BANK CEO: The frozen yogurt? Sure, my kids love that stuff.

LOAN OFFICER: Yes, well there's a danger these frozen yogurt companies are going to eat into the ice cream market in a big way. I'm worried that Jolliwhip might lose market share and have trouble making their loan payments.

BANK CEO: You mean they might default?

LOAN OFFICER: Yes, Mr. Houston.

BANK CEO: What can we do about it?

LOAN OFFICER: Well, we could do a credit default swap with Fleessem & Selle.

BANK CEO: Really? I hate those guys.

LOAN OFFICER: Yessir, but they might be willing to take on the Jolliwhip loan risk in return for a monthly fee.

BANK CEO: Spell it out for me, Jones. You know I don't understand that stuff.

LOAN OFFICER: We pay them five hundred bucks a month for the duration of the loan. If Jolliwhip fails to make a payment and defaults on their loan, then Fleessem's pays us the full amount, $500,000, and takes the loan off our hands.

BANK CEO: What happens if Jolliwhip doesn't default and pays back the loan to us?

LOAN OFFICER: Nothing. But either way, Fleessem's keeps the fee money.

BANK CEO: What? That's, like, thirty grand over five years!

LOAN OFFICER: Yessir, but thirty grand in insurance is better than five hundred grand, if Jolliwhip defaults.

BANK CEO: Hmm. You got me there.

A credit default swap looks a lot like an insurance contract: just as I might go to an insurance company because I need protection from the risk of my being flooded, my bank might go to Fleessem's because it needs protection against my company going bust and not paying back our loan; in the trade, they'd say my bank is the **buyer of protection**, and Fleessem's is the **seller of protection**.

But there's a key difference between insurance and swaps. Insurance contracts usually agree to pay for damage done to property: if your roof falls in or your house floods, you get a check to pay for someone to fix the damage. In a CDS, when the borrower fails to pay interest, the seller of protection writes a check. But it doesn't end there. In return for the full value of the loan, the seller of protection *gets the loan itself.* It's as if my house flooded, but rather than giving me money to fix the place up, the insurance company gives me a check equal to the value of the home, and takes possession of the property.

This exchange—the money for the credit—is part of the reason CDSs have become so popular. Because even when a the borrower has defaulted, the credit may still be worth something.

If I fail to pay interest on my loan, Fleessem's has to pay my bank $500,000. But that doesn't mean they've lost all that money. Like bonds, loans can be traded in a secondary market, and Fleessem's may be able to find someone to buy my loan. An investor might believe that the ice cream market is just about to recover, and that she can turn Jolliwhip around. She might agree to buy my loan for half price. That makes Fleessem's a lot happier—they get $250,000 of their money back.

It's the fact that a loan has value in the secondary market that explains why CDSs have become so numerous and infamous: that secondary valuation allows you to do a credit default swap *without owning the loan*!

Remember my neighbor, Clara? She's still a bit ticked about the way I made money off her with that Thanksgiving turkey. She is convinced that Jolliwhip is going to go bust because of all this frozen yogurt competition, and she wants to make money off my misfortune. She got the idea of using a CDS at my July Fourth barbecue, where she met Ian, the i-banker.

IAN: I saw BuzzBerry opened up another outlet just up the street from here. Those guys are really taking over this town.

CLARA: Yeah, Jolliwhip is in danger of getting frozen out! I'd make a bet that in six months Paddy and Linda won't be making payments on that loan they took out. The interest is way too high.

IAN: My bank would take some of that action.

CLARA: Really? Isn't that illegal?

IAN: Not at all. You can bet on the success or failure of any loan or bond.

CLARA: How does that work?

IAN: We simply behave as though you are the bank making the loan. You think the loan is going to go bad, so you need to buy protection from me.

Say $500 a month. And when the loan goes bad,
I pay you.

CLARA: How much?

IAN: Well, it depends on the value of the loan in the secondary market. If it's worth 90 percent, then I pay you the difference: $50,000. If it's worth 50 percent, then I pay you $250,000. If it's worth nothing, then you get the whole half million.

CLARA: Really? For $500 a month, I have the chance of a half-million-dollar payout when those guys go bust?

IAN: That's right. But if they don't go bust, then you keep paying me until the loan matures. That's a cool thirty-five grand, baby!

CLARA: Don't call me baby.

IAN: Sorry.

If this looks like a side bet on my inability to service my loan, that's exactly what it is. Clara has found a way to bet that I'll fail to pay my interest, while Ian's bank is betting that I'll keep paying. These kinds of

bets are completely legal, and because they don't require either the seller or the buyer to own a loan or a bond, anyone can make them. All you need is someone to take the other side of the bet.

And there are plenty of people willing to do just that. Bankers and financiers put these kinds of deals together thousands of times a day, on swaps desks all over the world. Sometimes investors will bet one way on a credit with one counterparty, then turn around and bet the opposite way on the same credit with another counterparty—just in case things don't go their way. The result is that there can be hundreds, or even thousands, of CDS contracts derived from a single bond or loan—which is why CDSs are the most numerous and notorious derivatives of all.

Just to give you an idea of how much money is involved in the CDS market, there were $62.2 trillion of these swaps outstanding in 2007, just before the financial crisis struck.

That sounds like an incredible amount, but the amount of money that was actually paid out in these swaps was a tiny fraction of that number. Swaps represent agreements to pay large amounts of money in the case of default, but they generally don't cost anything to arrange, and in many cases, the only money that changes hands is that monthly insurance payment made by the buyer of protection. If things go wrong, of course, the amounts of cash involved can be enormous—but the financial crisis showed that because the people involved in these swaps are often betting both ways, the transactions frequently cancel each other out. For example, financiers wrote $400 billion in CDSs on Lehman Brothers, but when the bank finally went under, only about $7 billion was actually paid out.

There were no armored cars or bulging briefcases involved in these transactions. All of the payments were made with the click of a mouse or the push of a return key. Bottom line numbers at the finance companies involved either rose or fell without a single vault door swinging open. This may seem obvious: after all, most people use electronic methods to pay for things these days, whether it be settling a bar tab with a credit card or making monthly car payments by direct debit. Computers have made things quicker and easier for everyone. And it means they can do more business. Once banks got together to create a global computer network for their trading and banking activity, the amount of financial activity around the world exploded. Suddenly dollars and pounds and euros and yen were whizzing around the earth at an incredible rate.

It was hard to believe.

It was even harder to keep track of.

★ ★ ★

CHAPTER SIX

The Folding Stuff

Money, and How It Makes Its Way Around the World

Money is no longer what it used to be, thanks to the credit system that allows people to borrow from each other, and the computer networks that link us all together.

Money used to be something that you could physically hold in your hand, whether gold coins, silver ducats, or bundles of banknotes. We invented money because it's easier than using **barter**. Most of us know how barter works because most of us used this process in our youth, before our parents gave us pocket money. In the playground, if we wanted something that one of our playmates had, we had to find something that he or she was willing to take in trade.

> **PADDY:** Hey, Kev, wanna swap your yo-yo for my Slinky?
>
> **KEVIN:** Cool.

By swapping our possessions, Kevin and I both got what we were after: a new toy. But what if Kevin becomes bored with his yo-yo and wants to get rid of it, but already has a Slinky? He could take my Slinky and hope to trade it for a Lego. Unfortunately, there's a lot of uncertainty here—there may be kids who'd like to swap their Lego for something else, but they might not want a Slinky. In such a case, no one's happy.

Our predecessors realized the shortcomings of barter and invented a kind of go-between for different transactions: something that most people would accept in exchange for their goods that could, in turn, be exchanged for other goods at a later date. Money.

At first, money had to be worth something in its own right. Most societies adopted the convention that money should be easily transferable, transportable, and measurable. You had to be able to literally weigh its worth in your hand. Some societies used precious gems or beads. The people of the Yap Islands in the western Pacific used carved stone discs called *rai* as money. The discs were carved from quartz stone quarried on faraway islands. The scarcity of the raw stone, and the risk involved in fetching it, ensured the value of the currency.

Most of the discs used by the Yap people were small, many about an inch wide, but others were as much as twelve feet in diameter. The biggest of these discs, called *fei*, were hard to transport, so the islanders decided that moving them wasn't necessary. They often assumed ownership of the *fei*, regardless of their location. An American anthropologist, William Furness, wrote that one family on Yap was acknowledged to be tremendously wealthy because it owned a *fei* that many years before had sunk to the bottom of the sea. No one alive had ever seen the *fei*, but its existence and value, and thus the wealth of its owner, were unquestioned.

Other societies developed coins, which first appeared between 500 and 700 BC. A coin made of gold or silver had a certain current value (which is why some people called it **currency**): you knew that if someone gave you a gold coin for your prize pig, that coin would buy you a specific amount of grain from Farmer Jones across town. Or a year's worth of apple pies from Mrs. Miggins's pie shop. Or even another pig, if that's what you wanted. The point was, you could swap your prize pig for something—money— that you could then swap for whatever your heart desired.

The problem with money—and coinage in particular—was that transportable though it may have been, it was almost invariably heavy, bulky, and inconvenient. In turn, a coinage system was vulnerable to fraud and other abuses (is this coin really gold? Better sink my teeth into it, to be sure), and it was easy to steal. Indeed, money was often the cause of economic problems like inflation and deflation (more about those later), and, worst of all, it was inaccurate.

Over the years, people came up with various ways to cope with some or all of the inconveniences of coin money. Many of the solutions involved written pieces of paper, or **notes**, which guaranteed the person carrying the notes access to money, rather than giving them the money itself. One of the most famous examples of this kind of system was the one maintained in the Middle Ages by the Knights Templar.

Back in the thirteenth century, bandits and pirates plagued the roads and sea routes, and anyone who carried money with them over any kind of distance risked losing it. But the Templars had outposts all over Europe, which gave them the opportunity to provide travelers a unique service. If a nobleman wanted to take, say, a hundred gold coins from Paris to Constantinople, rather than carry it all with him in an easily stolen chest, he could leave it with the Paris branch of the Templars. They would give him a piece of paper attesting that he had indeed left that much gold with the Paris office. If the nobleman survived the dangerous journey to Constantinople, he could go to the Templar office in that city and withdraw the same amount of coin—minus a small handling fee, of course!

The paper that the nobleman carried was a kind of **promissory note**, or IOU, which looks a lot like what businesses call a **letter of credit** today. It told the Knights Templar in Constantinople that they owed the bearer a hundred gold coins, and the bearer could cash in the note any time he liked. The note was such a simple, convenient idea that it didn't take long for it to catch on; very soon, banks began popping up all over Europe offering the same kinds of services as the Templars', issuing these IOUs to businesspeople and travelers.

People soon figured out that they could conduct all kinds of commerce with these pieces of paper. A man who deposited ten gold coins with a banking company could use his IOU as currency. To buy a horse, for example:

NOBLEMAN: That is a beautiful stallion. How much is he?

DEALER: Just ten gold coins to you, m'lord.

NOBLEMAN: Sounds a bit steep, old boy!

DEALER: He's good breeding stock, and worth every penny, sir.

NOBLEMAN: Well, I don't have that kind of coin on me right now, but I do have this note for ten gold coins from Beale's of Stratford.

> **DEALER:** Note?
>
> **NOBLEMAN:** Yes! Look, I'll sign it here, you bring it to them, and they'll give you the coin.
>
> **DEALER:** Hmm.

You can see why the dealer might not like the idea of a note—for starters, you can't sink your teeth into a piece of paper to see if it's genuine. In order to get his hands on his coin, the farmer would have to trek the ten miles down to Stratford and cash in the note. He'd have to buy lunch, his horse might throw a shoe . . . and what if he discovers the bank has gone bust once he arrives?

Despite all the possible downsides of using notes, they became very popular with businesspeople, especially those involved in complicated transactions using large amounts of money.

Promise to Pay

The Chinese invented a kind of banknote even before the Templars did—as early as the seventh century. As in Europe, and, later, America, each note supposedly represented a very specific amount of a commodity—silk, copper, silver, or gold. Each note had a promise written on it, avowing that the bearer could take the note to the bank and exchange it for a certain amount of the specified commodity. Some notes still say something very similar: British banknotes, for example, bear the words "I promise to pay the bearer the sum of [insert number] pounds."

Once people got used to the idea of using paper money, business became a lot easier to do—as long as one used the *right* money. Some banks, and even some countries, kept enough gold or silver in their vaults to make good on every promise written on every note they issued. Other countries started doing business that way but soon began issuing more notes without reserving any additional precious metal. This was a risky endeavor: if everyone wanted their gold at the same time, the countries'

"Just one pint of milk today, please!"

banks wouldn't be able to pay them. When people began to realize this, the value of the notes fell sharply and the prices of goods rose. This is what's called **inflation**.

The upside of having enough gold in one's vaults to redeem every note is that everyone has confidence in the value of the money—it's **as good as gold**. The downside is that raising more money is hard to do: one needs to find more gold to issue more notes, and the more one needs the gold, the more expensive it becomes.

When a currency becomes more expensive, a couple of things happen. First, the price of goods falls. When this happens, people who have gold tend to hoard it, so the currency becomes even more expensive, and that drives down the price of goods further still. This is what's called **deflation**. Deflation is great at first: Cars are cheaper! Toys are cheaper! Food is cheaper! But pretty soon the scorpion of deflation shows the sting in its tail. Investors become reluctant to invest in anything that is losing value day after day, so they stop putting their money into companies and they begin selling their shares. This is what economists call a **deflationary spiral**.

Imagine a toy store called Toyland. Toyland specializes in dolls, and the storekeeper has an inventory of thousands of dolls, in all colors, shapes, and sizes. All is well in Toyland until the day a dastardly technology company introduces a new handheld computer device that has virtual dolls on it. Kids go wild for the device, and quit playing with dolls overnight. Disaster! Toyland's owner has to offload several thousand of his dolls and buy accessories for the computer, quick. He cuts his prices. Unfortunately, he's not the only doll retailer in the town. There are dozens of stores, all trying to get rid of their dolls, and all cutting their prices. Toyland's owner wants to hold on to a few hundred dolls, as he knows there will always be some doll lovers out there, but as the other toy sellers hold huge sales, Toyland's owner can only watch in dismay as the value of his doll stock plunges. His accountant tells him he needs to sell all of his dolls, now, before they become worthless. So Toyland sets about slashing its prices, too.

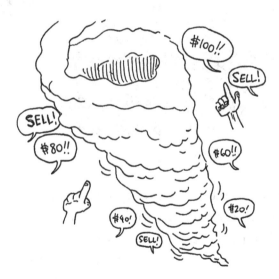

This is called **selling pressure**, and it's exactly what happens to company shares in a deflationary spiral. Investors sell some of their shares and buy something presumed to be a **safe haven**, like gold or treasury bonds. If enough investors sell, and there aren't many buyers, the price of shares falls. Other investors worry that their shares will be worth less the next day, so they sell their holdings, too. Pretty soon, everyone's selling: no one wants to buy something that in two weeks will be worth less than the amount they paid for it. In this situation, investors are only interested in safe havens. They're scared about what will happen to their money if they buy shares or make loans, so they do neither. Without investment, companies stop growing. They cut back, lay people off, and stop buying from other companies. Before long, the entire economy is in danger of being plunged into a **depression**.

From the moment the first currency was created, governments have battled the twin terrors of inflation and deflation by issuing what's called **fiat** currency. This means banknotes are worth a certain amount by government order, or fiat. In other words, it's the government saying, "This note is worth $20 for no reason other than the fact that we say it is." Fiat currencies have been around for centuries, but it wasn't until the U.S. government decided to make the dollar a fiat currency in 1972 that almost the entire world decided to adopt a similar system.

Once most of the world decided to adopt banknotes and fiat currencies, money became quite easy to work with, but it didn't conquer those twin terrors entirely. That's because most modern economies are founded on two essential truths. The first is that companies operate entirely in their own interest. And the second is that people are greedy.

Picture a man with ten children. He moves to a small town in the country that has just one store, which sells stuff that people in the country need, like hammers and tarps and animal feed. The McGivens store has some candy, but not much, because there aren't that many kids in the town.

The newcomers' kids love candy, however, and the first thing they do when they arrive is go exploring in the town, to see what they can buy with their pocket money. Rose, the eldest, leads the procession, and it doesn't take them long to find the McGivens store.

CHILDREN (IN UNISON):	Hello, mister!
MR. MCGIVENS:	Good heavens! Where did you lot spring from?
ROSE:	We've come from Chicago.
MR. MCGIVENS:	Well, that's a long way away.
ROSE:	Yes it is, and we're hungry.
CHILDREN:	We want candy!
MR. MCGIVENS:	Well, I don't have much in the way of candy here. I have some Red Strings and some lemon chews, and a big jar of hard candies. What would you like?
ROSE:	We've each got $2 in pocket money, so that's $20 altogether. How much are the hard candies?

Mr. McGivens thinks for a moment. Usually he charges five cents a candy, because so few people want to buy them. But today the situation has changed. Now there is suddenly a lot more candy money in the town, and only one place to spend it: his shop. An opportunity has presented itself.

Mr. McGivens:	The hard candies are eight cents each. The lemon chews are ten cents.
Rose:	Okay. We'll take a hundred lemon chews and . . . 125 hard candies, please. Here's $20.
Mr. McGivens:	Here's your candy.
Children (in unison):	Thank you!

They march out of the shop, just as Henry Tomkins enters.

Henry Tomkins:	Afternoon, John.
Mr. McGivens:	Afternoon, Henry.
Henry Tomkins:	I need a new shovel and a bag of fertilizer, please. And I'll take a dozen of those lemon chews.
Mr. McGivens:	That's $30 for the shovel, $25 for the fertilizer, and a dollar twenty for the candy.
Henry Tomkins:	A dollar twenty? They were sixty cents yesterday!
Mr. McGivens:	Sorry, Henry. Inflation.

The problem with inflation is that it makes your money worth less. Mr. McGivens's store is a micro economy that has been flooded by the children's candy money. The introduction of their $20 has doubled the price of the candy that Henry Tomkins likes to buy, or in other words his dollar can only buy half the candy it was able to buy the previous day. His dollar, then, has been devalued by 50 percent.

But inflation isn't all bad. In fact, governments quite like inflation—in moderation. Inflation may devalue existing currencies a little bit, but that can be offset by the fact that there's a lot more money coming into the system: money to spend, or invest, or build, or even hire more staff. So, in moderation, inflation can help keep people employed.

Take Mr. McGivens. Now that's he's making a bit more money from his candy, he has to think about how to use those profits. He could spend the money. Or he could plow it back into his business. Either way, that keeps the money in the system. Say he spends the money on a new tie for himself. That helps the retailer who sells him the tie, plus the tie makers, and the silk growers: there's a whole chain reaction through the tie business that can help keep people employed. In plowing the money back into his business, Mr. McGivens could refurbish his store, which would help local lumber suppliers and building workers. Or he could hire someone to help him with a stock count one day a week. That would give that employee an income, some of which she would likely spend, again sending positive, job-sustaining ripples through Mr. McGivens's hometown.

GOUGING VS. INFLATION ➤

Some people might accuse Mr. McGivens of **gouging**, but that's something quite different. Gouging happens when there is a **scarcity of goods**, with lots of demand, and the seller takes advantage of the scarcity to jack up prices.

In this case, there's no scarcity: Mr. McGivens has plenty of candies but he can see that the children have plenty of pocket money, too. That means they feel wealthier, and they're more willing to pay a little more for their treats.

Inflation, then, is part of our financial world, a necessary evil that most modern governments believe is best handled by fiat currency. But while the introduction of fiat currency seemed to be the answer to so many of government's fiscal problems, big business still wasn't entirely happy. Money may have become less volatile; it may have weighed a lot less, but it was just as cumbersome and unwieldy. Money still had to be counted up by one bank, transported by unreliable human beings, and then counted again at another bank. The chances of money being stolen were just as high as if it were coin, which is why businesspeople always preferred to do deals without involving physical money at all.

Many did so by using banks. This wasn't a new idea: businesspeople have used banks for centuries. The system is pretty simple. A grain buyer might have an account with one bank, and a grain seller might have an account with another bank. The buyer and seller would get together, agree on a price of five hundred florins for a thousand barrels of grain, and then notify their banks. Then they'd leave it up to the banks to make sure the money made it from one account to the other. That way neither buyer nor seller needed to sully their hands with money, and the banks took all the risk of transporting the cash.

This system existed for hundreds of years, and it still wasn't that efficient by the time the U.S. dollar became a fiat currency. Deals of all kinds needed lots of human beings adding up numbers and entering them in account ledgers. Agreements made by letter, telegraph, or even over the phone at banks and trading houses weren't any quicker, either, as they had to be verified by so-called **back-office** staff. Checks and other kinds of paperwork had to be mailed first, and then verified and cleared by clerical employees at either end, so the process took even longer. Everything had to be signed and stamped and dated, and kept in enormous filing cabinets.

When the idea of using fast, efficient computers instead of humans came along in the 1980s, bankers promoted the technology as quicker, easier, and safer. Not everyone was convinced by these arguments, and they pointed out that computers were just as vulnerable to thieves as a wagon loaded with gold coins.

Convenience and speed won the day, however, and the system has now become streamlined to the point that cash money is almost an abstraction. Gone are the days when companies, or even banks, would demand truckloads of banknotes or wagons of gold from each other to settle accounts. Pretty much the only reason banks have cash anymore is to fill ATM machines for the public's use. Which makes sense, when you think of fiat currency: if a government can give value to a scrap of paper, then surely it can give value to a number in an electronic account.

Money has now become so easy to use that we can transport billions in currency over thousands of miles in mere seconds. Even so, the creation of money has become a bit more difficult. When money was minted from a commodity like gold, all you had to do to make a coin was melt down a chunk of metal, form a coin shape, and hammer a design onto it. Today, creating money requires the smooth cooperation of the government and an entire network of banks, whose business is built on borrowing money on the one hand, and lending it out on the other. The creation of money in American society is a delicate, almost magical process, and without the banks, money as we know it would not exist today.

CHAPTER SEVEN

The House Always Wins

The Banking System

The word **bank** means different things to different people. To some, a bank is a place to go to borrow money. To others it's a secure place to keep their savings.

Just as humans learn to borrow and lend from each other as they grow up, so the banks existed first to lend money. In fact, they were probably lending currency long before money was even invented. It wasn't until the time of the ancient Greeks and Romans that bankers hit on the idea of taking deposits in as well as lending money out. Up until then, if you had any spare cash, you either carried it on your person or kept it locked away in your house.

Rome, seventh century BC. A warm day in late spring. Two bankers meet by the Porta Saturni.

QUICKUS BUCCHUS:	Good morning, Voluminus! Who are these men with you today?
VOLUMINUS BONUS:	They're bodyguards, Quickus. Don't tell me you haven't heard about the thieves roaming the city?

QUICKUS BUCCHUS:	Ah, yes, Sicilians, I'm told. Dangerous chaps. Good thing you built that vault for all your gold last year.
VOLUMINUS BONUS:	Hmph. I wish I could make enough money to fill it.
QUICKUS BUCCHUS:	Here's an idea. Now that everyone in Rome is petrified of having their coin pinched from under their pillows in the middle of the night, why not offer to store their money for them?
VOLUMINUS BONUS:	Why on earth would I want to do that?
QUICKUS BUCCHUS:	Because then you could lend it out to people like that merchant Graspus. I heard he borrowed five hundred gold coins to equip a ship, took it to Africa, and came back with a hold full of spices that he sold for four thousand.
VOLUMINUS BONUS:	Four thousand!
QUICKUS BUCCHUS:	Crazy, right? Who wouldn't want a piece of that action?
VOLUMINUS BONUS:	Tell me more about this idea of yours.
QUICKUS BUCCHUS:	You promise to keep your clients' gold safe and guarded in your vault. Except that you don't. You turn around and lend it out again.
VOLUMINUS BONUS:	But what if all those people want their money back?
QUICKUS BUCCHUS:	All at the same time? Not likely! Especially not with those Sicilians around; they'll want to keep it safe. No, you keep ten or twenty percent of it in the vault, to be sure that you can give out a few coins here or there when people ask for it. But the rest goes straight to chaps like Graspus. Next thing you know, you're rolling in dough.
VOLUMINUS BONUS:	But those Sicilians aren't going to be around for-

ever. When they leave, will people still want to keep their cash safe with me?

QUICKUS BUCCHUS: Tell you what, cut me in, and I'll have a word with the Sicilians. See if we can't keep them around for a little while longer!

Bankers quickly realized they could make tidy profits by investing the money that their customers had deposited with them. They needed to keep a certain amount of money on hand, in case any of their customers wanted a little cash quickly, but they could lend the rest out for a steady rate of interest. Of course, it can't have been long before customers saw the banks were making a nice living this way, and decided they wanted a piece of the action.

CANONUS RUSTICUS: Morning, Voluminus Bonus.

VOLUMINUS BONUS: Canonus! How well you look! The life of a farmer suits you, I can see. You're in town for the market?

CANONUS RUSTICUS: I am. Got a nice stack of silver for my pigs this year.

VOLUMINUS BONUS: Delighted to hear it. How much will you be depositing?

CANONUS RUSTICUS: Well, that depends. I hear you've been making quite a tidy profit, using my money to invest in the spice trade.

VOLUMINUS BONUS: I, ah . . . ahem.

CANONUS RUSTICUS: Look, it's fine with me, so long as my money's available to me when I want it. But if you want me to keep depositing my silver with you, I want something in return. Say two percent interest on the cash I keep in your vault.

VOLUMINUS BONUS: But I'm only making . . .

CANONUS RUSTICUS: You're making plenty, Voluminus, and you can afford to pay me a little share of whatever you're getting for lending out my money to Graspus Opportunitus, or whoever it is you're dealing with. I want two percent—or I could just carpe diem, and go across the street to Creditus Unionus . . .

And with that, the bank took on two roles, and became both a borrower and a lender. Today most banks work this way, borrowing money from depositors at one rate of interest, and lending the money out again at another, higher rate of interest. And pocketing the difference.

You might think that makes bankers pretty selfish. They pay measly rates of interest to their depositors and charge higher rates to people who want to borrow from them. In the end they're firmly focused on making a profit for themselves and their shareholders. The loans they make are a way to make that money.

Fortunately, the banks' lust for profits works to everyone's advantage. The loans the banks make to companies and people usually do a great deal of good. The money helps us to buy everything from groceries to cars and houses, and it helps companies expand and hire. If people are able to borrow (and don't overstretch), the money they borrow can help grow businesses and create jobs, and that's good for everyone.

There's another benefit to banks' desire to lend money out in order to make profits: Lending *creates* money. Out of thin air!

This is how the magic works. One day, Mr. Smith comes to his bank and deposits $1 million. The bank keeps 10 percent, or $100,000, in reserve, in case Mr. Smith wants some of his money quickly.

The next day, Mrs. Jones comes to the same bank and asks for a $900,000 loan, to buy a private jet. The bank lends her the money. Suddenly the amount of money in the system has almost doubled. There's the million dollars that Mr. Smith has in his bank account. And there's

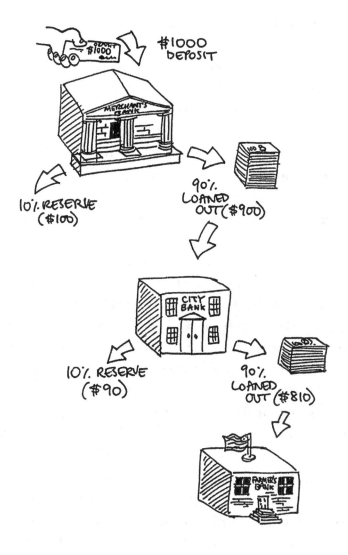

the $900,000 loan the bank made to Mrs. Jones. Both are assets—Mr. Smith can point to his million-dollar balance on his statement, and Mrs. Jones has a briefcase full of cash—so both are real. The bank has turned a million dollars into $1.9 million, just like that.

Mrs. Jones drives out of the airport and gives the briefcase full of cash to Mr. Sharif, of Sharif Aviation. Mr. Sharif gives Mrs. Jones the keys to a gently used Bell 407 helicopter and puts the cash in his bank. The bank puts 10 percent ($90,000) aside as a reserve and lends $810,000 to a clothing manufacturer who needs to buy some new equipment. The clothing maker gives the equipment salesman the $810,000. He takes it to his bank, which holds 10 percent in reserve, and . . .

You get the picture. That $1 million has now more than tripled, in terms of its purchasing power. And yet there's no *new* money in the system—it's still just a million dollars. It's the banks' ability to lend that money out, over and over, that creates a ripple effect through the economy and improves everyone's ability to spend and to grow. Lending and borrowing can be a good thing, in other words. So long as you don't overdo it.

Which means that banks aren't all bad. Yes, some banks—or the bankers who run them—do make mistakes. Some bankers cheat, some bankers lie, and some bankers take foolish risks that threaten the entire global economy. But most banks and bankers work to our mutual benefit, and the network of the country's banks has become an essential part of our economy, driving money through the system like a heart pumping blood around the body.

Many people feel as though the financial system operates in a different world to the one we live in, but in fact it has become an integral part of our lives. Through our interaction with our bank, most of us have some kind of dealing with the system every day, whether it be depositing money, writing a check, making an ATM withdrawal, or using a credit card. Many of us interact with our banks more than with our own relatives. The relationship we have with our bank is important, which is why we're so choosy about which bank we go to. Some people want to be able to do business with a person, so they contract with a bank with lots of branches. Others want quick access, so they sign up with a bank with lots of ATM machines. Or there are those who do a lot of business online, so they plump for a bank with the best Web platform. The relationships we have with our banks all have different demands, but there is one common requirement: trust.

We trust our banks to be efficient. We trust our banks to live up to the terms of their relationship with us. We trust them to make loans to people who will pay interest regularly, and pay the money back when the loan matures. We trust them to be able to give us our money back when we need it. It's why so many banks in America have the word *trust* in their name.

Sometimes banks show they cannot be trusted. They can, and do, make bad investments. In the U.S. savings and loan crisis of the 1980s and 1990s, banks lent far too much to doomed real estate projects that failed to make any money. In the years leading up to the financial crisis, banks bought mortgage bonds that were critically flawed and almost guaranteed to fail. In both cases, once people heard that their bank had made foolish investments, they tried to get their money back.

As Quickus Bucchus pointed out earlier, when a handful of people go to the bank and ask for their money, the bank can usually handle it, thanks to the money they're required to hold in reserve. When everyone wants their money back, however, it's a problem. When a large number of depositors do this at once, it's called a **bank run** (or a **run on the bank**). Why a bank run? Probably because in the old days (that's before everyone had a telephone), if you heard a bank was making bad investments, the only way to get your money out was to run down there and try to get to the front of the line that was inevitably forming. And a few people hastening through the financial district could soon turn into a full-blown stampede.

Today you can demand your money back with a click of a mouse, so you don't need to form a line outside the bank. But many people still do, assuming that the bank will have hard cash in its vault. But whether people are lining up in person or demanding withdrawals online, it can cause big problems for the bank involved. As we've seen, most banks only have a small proportion of their total deposits on reserve. To get more cash, they need to sell, or **liquidate**, investments. That can take time, and the bank may end up taking a loss—just like selling a house or a car, the more quickly you have to sell, the less you're likely to get a high price.

A MODERN-DAY BANK RUN ➤

Those who thought the computer age had put an end to old-style bank runs were given a rude awakening on June 27, 2008.

Customers of the Southern California lender IndyMac began lining up outside the bank to withdraw their money. Many were spooked by rumors of a letter written by Senator Chuck Schumer (D- NY) warning that IndyMac would be left vulnerable if large numbers of depositors withdrew their cash.

Depositors took out $730 million online and in person over the following week. The bank's stock plunged to near zero. IndyMac was so weakened that it was forced to lay off more than half its staff. On July 11 the government stepped in and took IndyMac over.

Bank runs have happened so many times that they make numerous appearances in the plots of Hollywood films, from *It's a Wonderful Life* in 1946 to *Too Big to Fail* in 2011. So many banks have failed, in fact, that the government has created an insurance plan to deal with the problem. In 1933, following the great stock market crash of 1929, the government formed the **Federal Deposit Insurance Corporation** (FDIC). The FDIC insures accounts, up to a certain amount, held in banks that have signed up for the plan. It's what banks call a **backstop**, and it's there to bolster your trust in the bank's guarantee that your money is safe. Most financial advisors recommend banking with institutions that are part of the FDIC program. That's comparatively easy, as most American banks have signed up with the FDIC, but some online and foreign banks don't participate. It's easy to check, however. Banks advertise their membership on their websites and in their lobbies, and consumers can check with one phone call.

The government created the FDIC, but in the event the program has to make a payout to customers, the cash comes solely from the dues paid in by the banks in the plan. The FDIC insures *our* money, not the banks', but the fact that the government saw a need to protect banks from any crisis in consumer confidence shows how important it thinks the banking system is.

Up to now, we've been talking about **commercial banking**, which is the business of lending to companies, and the job of taking deposits from, and lending money to, individuals—also called **retail banking**. Most of the local banks that you find on the main street of your city or town confine themselves to commercial banking, lending to local people and local firms. But many of the big national and regional banks also get involved in another kind of banking business, called **investment banking**.

Investment Banking

Investment banks are involved in so-called **capital markets** activities, the capital markets being the bond and stock markets. When you want to raise money in those markets, you go to an investment bank for help. Investment banks also get involved in the trading of stocks and bonds and other securities, and they often specialize in **asset management**, where they advise wealthy people and moneyed organizations how to invest. The banks often do the buying and selling for those clients, too. Finally, many investment banks advise companies on **mergers and acquisitions**

(M&As), helping them decide what competitors to buy, or partner with, and then assisting them in doing those deals.

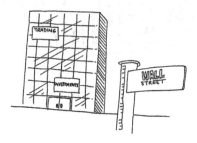

Investment banks don't have branches. If you try to find a branch of Goldman Sachs in your city, for example, you'll be searching for a long time. There are no main street outlets, no tellers, and no ATMs. Investment banks generally don't take deposits, so they can't make money from the business of borrowing from depositors at one rate and lending the same money out at a higher rate in the way that a Main Street bank does. Instead, investment banks mainly make money in two ways: from trading and by charging fees.

Want someone to help you with a bond issue or to sell some stock? There's a fee for that. What about some advice on what securities to buy for your portfolio? There's a fee for that, too. Want to do a merger or buy a competitor? Yep: it'll cost you! These banks often charge a fee when they buy and sell securities for their clients, and they also use their own money to trade—hoping to make substantial profits in the process. You've probably heard of some of these investment banks: Goldman Sachs and Morgan Stanley are two big ones; Lehman Brothers and Bear Stearns were two investment banks that became infamous for their role in the 2008 financial crisis. Not all investment banks are as big or as famous as Goldman Sachs. Many are small and specialized. They're often referred to as **boutiques**, and they usually focus on very specific areas of business, such as movie financing, or telecommunications.

THE BANKING ACT OF 1933 ➤

Commonly referred to as the Glass-Steagall Act because its main sponsors were Senator Carter Glass (D-VA) and Congressman Henry B. Steagall (D-AL).

The act was introduced in reaction to a period of deflation, which resulted from the depression that followed the great stock market crash of 1929. In those days, there was little distinction between what we would today call commercial bankers, and brokers, people who dealt in the capital markets. Hearings revealed all sorts of conflicts of interest and fraud in banking, and Glass and Steagall resolved to separate the two activities.

The act also created the Federal Deposit Insurance Corporation (FDIC).

Those parts of the Glass Steagall Act that separated investment and commercial banking were repealed by the Gramm-Leach-Bliley Act of 1999, signed into law by President Clinton.

From 1933, when the **Glass-Steagall Act** was passed, until 1999, commercial banks were not allowed to do capital markets business, and investment banks were forbidden from doing retail banking business. Regulators were concerned that if a commercial bank decided to do some investment banking business and lost a lot of money, it could threaten the deposits of its retail clients. But in 1999, the government decided that banks could be trusted to regulate themselves in this area, and the repeal of provisions in the Glass-Steagall Act allowed banks to do both types of business. Which is why if you ask your bank what kind of business it does, you may find that it's a commercial bank and an investment bank—all rolled up into one.

Banks are a bit like cars. The basic ones, like my granny's powder-blue Mini Clubman, just have an engine, four wheels, and a steering system. In the banking system, these basic models are the local retail banks, the companies that take deposits and make loans and do little else. As you move up the car market, you get some add-ons like ABS or halogen lights, perhaps some more horsepower. The same goes for the banking market. Regional banks offer mortgage products and investment advice. Some have credit cards and rewards programs. At the top of the system you have the national banks, the huge SUVs of the system, and their otherworldly cousins, the investment banks. In the car world, investment banks are like military transport vehicles. They have four wheels and an engine, but the similarity ends there—they're not for consumer use at all.

But whether they're investment banks, commercial banks, or pure retail banks, all banks have one thing in common: they all lend money to each other in what's called the **interbank lending market**. The loans are made over short periods, just a week or less. Many loans are made for less than twenty-four hours, in what's called the **overnight market**. This is particularly common at the upper levels of the banking system, where the big Wall Street commercial and investment banks operate. One bank might have an unexpected need for cash, perhaps to pay clients who are cashing out in larger numbers than usual, while another might have a surplus acquired from a particularly good trading day. Rather than sitting on that surplus, the bank with the cash can decide to hire it out for a night and get a small amount of money in return. The overnight market is also called the **repo market**, because the loans aren't technically loans at all, but **repurchase agreements**, or repos.

THE REPO MARKET ➤

In a repo transaction, a bank that needs money "sells" some bonds or other securities to a counterparty institution. The sale comes with an agreement that the bank will buy back, or repurchase, the securities at a later date.

The repurchase price will be slightly more than the original sale price, so that **the repo is effectively a loan**, with that little bit of extra money acting as the interest.

Whether you call it the interbank lending, repo, or overnight market, the lending market between banks is highly **liquid**, in that there are always banks with a bit of extra cash to lend, and there are always banks who need a helping hand, for one reason or another. If the banking system is like the engine of the economy, the interbank market is like an oil pump, and the cash that's pumped from bank to bank each night and back again the next day is like the lubricant that keeps the various and distant parts of the mechanism moving smoothly.

No matter how complex or simple the banks may be, they all need a regular checkup—just as cars do. In the banking system, the mechanics that do the monitoring and conduct the checks are the **regulators**, and there are a lot of them. Commercial banks, which handle the paychecks and loans of most Americans, are quite heavily regulated. They get a lot of support from the government, but in return they are checked out a lot more frequently and more thoroughly. They can't take huge risks in the capital markets and they have to hold a lot of money in reserve, in case things go wrong. Investment banks are much more lightly regulated.

Many people argue that there are too many regulators, and that they often contradict each other. That may be so, but the reason the regula-

tory system was created was to protect the enormous network of banks in this country, and, of course, to protect all the people who have entrusted their earnings and savings to the banking system. With such an array of banks, all doing different kinds of business, the banking system is highly complicated, even chaotic. From the outside, it looks a bit like a pile of building blocks, stacked up by a rather creative child. The construction is random, multicolored, made up of blocks of all shapes and sizes. And at the heart of it all lies the most important block, the foundation of the entire structure, and the most important component of the entire system. In the real world, that base component is the government's bank, the bank that directs all of the government's money into the system; it is the central bank, which can change the size and shape and even the conduct of the Byzantine structure that it supports. That bank is called the **Federal Reserve**.

CHAPTER EIGHT

Loosening the Beltway

The Fed, the Treasury, and How Government Gets Involved

The Federal Reserve isn't just one bank: it's a system of banks, twelve in all, located all around the country, and overseen by a committee based in Washington, D.C.

The Fed, as it's often called, is separate from the **Department of the Treasury**, although the two work closely together and are often confused. News headlines might refer to "the government" printing money, selling government bonds, adjusting interest rates, buying government bonds, or pumping money into the banking system, but it's often unclear to ordinary people whether it's the Treasury or the Fed that's doing the buying, selling, printing, or pumping.

The Fed and the Treasury both deal with the country's money, but in very different ways. In simple terms, they're both responsible for the flow of money through the United States through its public and private arteries. One artery, the Treasury, carries the money that's in the government's account. That cash is distributed across America, into the pocketbooks of people and the bottom lines of companies, via federal programs and grants and spending by government agencies. The Treasury oversees how

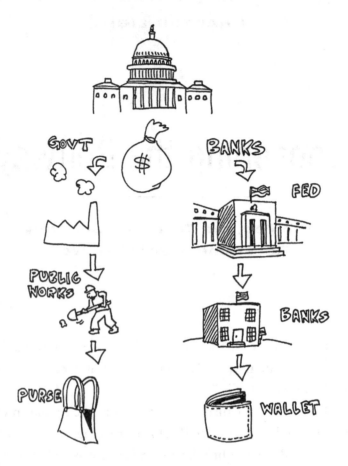

that money is spent and how it circulates back into the government coffers through taxes. The other artery, the Fed, pipes the money through the banking system, via interbank loans and loans that banks make to companies and consumers.

I like to think of the Treasury and the Fed as two characters in the Mafia movie *The Godfather*. There's a character in the film called Tom Hagen, the Godfather's key advisor, or consigliere. He advises the Corleone family about how they should run their operations—what to do to get money in the door, and how to spend that money most effectively. The Treasury secretary has a similar role in government. He doesn't make

any decisions about taxing and spending—only the Congress can make those decisions—but his Treasury is a fully integrated government department. Part of the family, if you will. The Treasury secretary advises the president and the Congress on the best way to manage the government purse—how much money to raise through taxation or through borrowing (by selling bonds) and how to distribute the cash through the economy in the form of government spending. Finally, the Treasury secretary acts as the agent of Congress—his department, which includes the Internal Revenue Service and the U.S. Mint, carries out Congress's decisions. Like the Godfather's consigliere, the Treasury secretary holds a very powerful and important position.

The Fed is just as influential, but in a different way. If the Treasury secretary is the government's consigliere, the Fed is a bit more like a character in *The Godfather* named Luca Brasi. Brasi is a hired gun. He's highly trusted by the Corleones, but he's not a family member. Still, the family gives Brasi a free hand in his "operations," trusting that he will always act in the best interest of the Organization. The Fed operates in a similar way. The Fed's chairman and governors are appointed by the president and overseen by Congress, and the chairman has to check in with Congress frequently. Otherwise, however, the Fed is independent. It doesn't have to ask either the president or Congress for permission to do what it does, but it is always presumed to act in the interests of the country.

FISCAL VS. MONETARY POLICY ➤

Both the Fed and the Treasury have the ability to control the economy. But they have very different tools.

The Treasury is the agent of what's called **fiscal policy**. Fiscal policy is how the government, via the Treasury, uses taxes and spending to influence the economy.

The Fed is the agent of **monetary policy**. Monetary policy is the way the Fed controls the **money supply**—the amount of money that's in the banking system and how freely that money flows.

The Fed and the Treasury are restricted in that they only have a few tools to do their work. The Treasury uses **fiscal policy** to adjust tax rates, government spending, and the amount of money the government gets from borrowing by selling bonds. But it can't do any of those things without permission from the Congress. It's the politicians on Capitol Hill who decide which fiscal tools the Treasury can use, and how much it can use them.

My ice cream company, Jolliwhip, uses a kind of fiscal policy when it does business. My business partner Linda and I own the company, so we're a bit like the Congress. Terry, our chief operations officer, is also our accountant. He's the Treasury secretary. By now we have a franchise operation of a hundred trucks, selling our ice cream all over the state. The truck operators pay us a flat fee, like a tax, and a proportion of their profits. One day Terry gets us together.

TERRY: We are having a problem with our budget. The price of milk has gone through the roof. Plus, with winter coming on, the trucks are making less money. Which means we're making barely enough to cover our outgoings. Unless we're careful, we're going to go bust.

PADDY: Can't we just hike the franchise fee and get some more money in that way? Kind of like **raising taxes**?

TERRY: We could, but that will squeeze the franchisees. It might make them more cautious about ordering and taking on new routes. They might end up losing money and going out of business. Then we'd be in big trouble.

LINDA: If we're blowing our budget, we should **cut spending**. Maybe reduce the number of trucks we have out there; then we wouldn't have to make so much ice cream. Or maybe we cut costs by using less cream in the recipe.

PADDY: No way. It's the creaminess that makes our ice cream so popular. If we make cuts like that, people will stop buying our product and we'll go out of business.

LINDA: So what do you suggest?

PADDY: How about we **raise money** by taking out another loan from the bank? We could use the money to buy some more trucks and cover some new routes. We could make more money that way.

TERRY: We could do that, too, but the interest we're paying on our current loan is already pretty substantial. The new loan will have a higher rate, so we'll be paying more to service the debt. Even if the trucks do more business, they may not make enough.

LINDA: I don't like that idea. We could end up digging ourselves into a bigger hole. Why don't we try dropping the franchise fee, like a **tax cut**. Then the trucks will have more money for fuel, so they can drive some new routes and make more money that way.

TERRY: Maybe. We'd make less in fees, but we might make more in our share of the profits. But if the trucks don't make any more money, then we're still in a hole.

If Linda, Terry, and I are having a hard time figuring out the best way to balance our books, you can imagine what the Congress and the Treasury secretary have to cope with. We're merely running a small company; they have to figure out what fiscal policy approach is best for the entire U.S. economy. The tools they have are more like blunt instruments than scalpels: a tiny change in government expenditure or borrowing or taxes can have a big effect.

The Fed has a parallel role in keeping the economy shipshape, but its principal focus is on keeping unemployment low and holding prices steady—preventing **inflation** and **deflation**, which we learned about in chapter 6. The Fed has several **monetary policy** tools that it can use, and it can use them as much as it likes, and without asking Congress for permission. But just like the Treasury's fiscal measures of taxing, spending, and borrowing, the small adjustments the Fed makes to the money supply have big effects, so the Fed treads carefully.

Employment is one of the factors that the Treasury and the Federal Reserve care about most. If unemployment is rising, the Treasury might decide to tackle the problem using *fiscal* measures. It could cut taxes on corporations, believing that businesses will take the money they don't have to pay the government and use it to either hire more people or buy more goods. It could cut taxes on ordinary citizens, believing that people will then go out and shop, helping companies to grow and hire more people. Alternatively, Treasury could decide to spend money to deal with the problem, perhaps hiring more people into government departments, or maybe contracting companies to do work for the government, which would then push those companies to hire more people.

The **Federal Reserve** would use *monetary* measures to deal with the problem. To get people working, the Fed needs to get more money into the system: it's those extra dollars that will pay the workers' wages. But the Fed can't just walk around the country, handing out bags of cash to companies (or dropping them from helicopters, as Fed Chairman Ben Bernanke once said). It has to do things indirectly.

Earlier, I compared the Fed to Luca Brasi, a character in *The Godfather*. This is where I take the reins from Francis Ford Coppola and rewrite the script. Imagine Luca has become head of his own Organization, with operations all over the city. Each district is run by a captain, each of whom has a crew of street guys. The captains kick back a percentage of each crew's operations to Luca, but otherwise they're very independent. To stop the captains from going too crazy or getting any ideas, Luca requires them to keep 10 percent of their worth in a reserve account that Luca controls. That's not so bad, as Luca pays the captains a bit of interest on that money, and he lets them borrow from the reserve for next to nothing when they need a little extra short-term cash. They can even borrow longer-term from Luca, if they need to.

One day Luca gets a call from his wife's sister's niece's daughter. She tells Luca that her brother's cousin, who's a low-level street guy working on the docks, was overheard carping about his captain in a bar. Work has dried up, his captain seems to have slowed operations down, and the rank and file of the Organization aren't getting paid. The guys are unhappy.

It's an unsettling call: Luca and his advisors have been hearing similar things for several weeks. So Luca calls a meeting.

LUCA: Okay, guys, what's going on? Why aren't the crews working?

"SMILER" MORANT:	Well, boss, there has been a bit more police activity recently. Plus it's the winter. Business always slows down this time of year.
LUCA:	Yeah, but not this much. And police or no police, we have to get the guys earning. If they don't earn, we don't earn, and then everyone's unhappy. Do I need to call the captains in for a face-to-face?
SMILER:	Not yet. You could try a couple other things first. Have you noticed that the captains are holding quite a bit of cash in the reserve account? Much more than usual. Some of them have got forty percent of their worth in the kitty.
LUCA:	Why would they do that?
SMILER:	Because you're paying pretty good interest on that money. They probably figure they can make almost as much in interest by keeping that cash in the reserve as they can make on the street right now.
LUCA:	So what do I do? What d'you think. Crumbs?
"CRUMBS" PULASKI:	You gotta couple of options, boss. You can cut the interest rate on the account. If you make it so they're only getting half what they're getting now, that'll pressure them to put the money to work on the street.
LUCA:	Okay. What else?
CRUMBS:	You could cap the amount the captains can keep in the account. Tell them no more than ten percent. Then they'll have to look for ways to make money elsewhere.

Luca is concerned about the **money supply** in his Organization. If there's not enough money flowing through the system, then his captains aren't doing business, and his foot soldiers aren't getting paid. So he needs to find ways to **increase the money supply** in his own little criminal economy. Luca is just like the chairman of the Federal Reserve, who is focused on making sure the money supply in the economy is adequate to keep as many people as possible employed, without causing inflation.

The Fed's "captains" are America's banks: They're required to keep a certain amount on deposit at the Federal Reserve Bank. This reserve of cash is called the **federal funds account**, and it has two purposes. First, it's a kind of security cushion, so that if a bank runs out of money for any reason, it has a backup supply at the Fed. Second, the federal funds account is a pool of money that banks can borrow from each other, if they don't have enough to make up their **reserve requirement**. This borrowing activity occurs in what's called the **overnight market** because banks have to pay the money back the very next day. The interest rate at which the banks borrow from the federal funds account is called the **federal funds rate**, and because the loan durations are so short, the rate is usually very low.

Unfortunately for the Fed, it can't change interest rates as easily as our mob boss. The banks really decide the rate themselves, charging each other marginally different rates to borrow overnight. The average rate of those transactions is called the **federal funds *effective* rate**. But the Fed does try to influence the rate, by issuing guidance, in what it calls the **federal funds target rate**.

The target rate is more than just a pie-in-the-sky wish. The Fed can influence the rate by using so-called **open market operations**. When it uses open market operations, the Fed behaves a bit like a big sponge. Squeeze the sponge, and liquid flows out. Let the sponge relax, and it sucks the liquid back up. Except with the Fed, it's money that flows back and forth.

SETTING THE TARGET RATE ➤

The Fed chairman doesn't set the target rate alone. Every two months or so, he meets with a division of the Federal Reserve called the **Federal Open Markets Committee (FOMC).**

The FOMC consists of twelve advisors. Seven are the members of the Federal Reserve Board, and the other five are chairs of one of the dozen regional Federal Reserve Banks.

Together, the FOMC comes to an agreement on what they would *like* the federal funds rate to be. Hence the target rate.

The key to the efficient working of the Federal Reserve's sponge is the network of **primary dealers** in the banking system. Primary dealers are banks that have committed to make a market in government bonds. In fact they buy most of the bonds that the government sells, and then sell those bonds on to the public. It's a lucrative, privileged position, in return for which these banks have to sell bonds back to the Fed when it asks them to, and they have to buy bonds whenever the Fed says under a system of **repurchase agreements**, or **repos**. There are roughly twenty-one primary dealers in the United States banking system, which makes them a small, exclusive group. They're a bit like the most favored captains in our mafia Organization, the guys the boss knows he can rely on in a pinch.

Back to the sponge, which we now see isn't just the twelve banks in the Federal Reserve system but also the entire network of primary dealer banks. One day, the Fed looks around the country and sees unemployment is rising. Clearly, there needs to be more money in the system, so it's time to squeeze the sponge. First, the Fed releases the new target fed funds rate, which is 1 percent lower than the current fed funds effective rate. Then it's time to squeeze:

FED: All right, you deadbeats! I'm calling in my repos. Here's fifty billion dollars, now gimme back my bonds!

BULGEBANC: Great. We're fifty billion dollars more liquid. But what are we supposed to do with all this cash?

GRASPCOR: Well, we can't keep it here. No one's borrowing from Fed funds right now. There's too much money in the system.

HORDINC: Forget this. My money's making bubkes just sitting in the federal funds account. I'll get a better return lending to homebuyers in Washington State.

MISECO: I'm going to lend to entrepreneurs in Raleigh, North Carolina.

BULGEBANC: Great idea, guys! Either of you need a partner?

One tiny squeeze, and the federal funds pool is suddenly swimming in money. Now those banks that have to borrow in the overnight market to make their reserve requirements can get the money they need much more cheaply. That pushes the effective fed funds interest rate down, so that no one's making much money from lending in the pool anymore. So the banks look for different investments: in real estate, restaurants, industry, wherever. With that, the money supply in the system increases. Companies find they can borrow money more cheaply, so they buy more, build more, hire more. People go back to work, and because interest rates are low, they see little point in saving much of their paycheck. So they spend money, which helps companies grow, and the virtuous cycle of capitalism turns in everyone's favor . . .

. . . until the Fed wakes up one day and sees that there's too much money in the system. Credit is too cheap; it's too easy to get a loan; prices are rising too fast. The Fed calls a meeting of the FOMC, which decides to *raise* the federal funds target rate. To get the effective rate up to the target, the Fed uses its sponge to suck up some of the cash in the system.

FED: All right, ladies and gentlemen, line up! Come on and get your bonds—safer than having all that cash lying about, but just as liquid as regular greenbacks. Plus my bonds pay interest. Get 'em while they're hot!

BULGEBANC: Phew! It's about time! I'm in cash up to my ears. Gimme a billion dollars' worth.

GRASPCOR: Tell me about it. I'm not getting much more from lending to developers in Tampa than I am from lending to you! I'll take two bil.

HORDINC: I'll take a billion. Now I can push up interest rates on homeowners—property prices have gone nuts in Seattle.

MISECO: All right, Fed. A billion it is. I'm still gonna be able to lend to entrepreneurs in Raleigh, though. Even at a percentage point higher. Those guys are burning cash!

GRASPCOR: Hmm. Raleigh, eh? Do I have any branches there?

Now the prime dealer banks have got a truckload of bonds, and the Fed has got several billion dollars of the banks' money. And just like that, there's a lot less money in the federal funds pool. Now any bank that hasn't got enough cash to cover its reserve requirements will have to pay a bit more, pushing the federal funds rate upward. In turn, all the other interest rates rise, as the banks pass on the cost of borrowing to companies, who pass it on to customers. Those rising interest rates discourage borrowing by companies and individuals. That means companies have less money to grow and less to spend. Higher interest rates also encourage individuals to save their money, rather than spend it, putting another brake on the economy. The Fed's hope is that if there's less money out there chasing goods and services, inflation will ease off a little.

Open market operations are the Federal Reserve's most-used tool in its efforts to control the money supply. Which is why you hear about the Fed buying and selling bonds all the time, often in large amounts. But sometimes open market operations don't work as well as the Fed would like. Sometimes, the Fed has to resort to other methods to get money moving around the system.

Back to Luca Brasi's office. Luca's advisors pointed out that he can vary the amount that the captains can keep in the reserve account. The Fed can do that, too. By insisting the banks keep only 10 percent of their assets in the federal funds pool, any excess cash has to look for an alternative investment. But sometimes that's not enough to get things going, either.

LUCA: I got another call from my sister-in-law's niece's daughter again, guys. She's a sweet girl, but she's driving me crazy. She says things aren't getting any better out there.

SMILER: Yeah, the captains are kinda skittish, boss. They heard about that FBI sting in Cincinnati. They're worried about doing business in this climate. They say it's too risky. Instead they're socking away money for their families, in case they get pinched.

LUCA: Those yellow-bellied sons 'a . . . Anyone got any ideas?

SMILER: Well, I can understand why they want to build a nest egg right now. We won't be able to stop them doing that. So we need to give them more money for their operations.

LUCA: Hand out dough to these guys? I'm not doing that!

CRUMBS: We're not saying you should give the money away, boss. But you could make it cheaper for them to borrow from you.

LUCA: Cheaper? I'll be chiseling myself!

CRUMBS: Hear me out. If they can borrow cheap, then their cost of business drops. If they don't get busted— and we all hope they don't—they'll make a lot more money on whatever deals they do. The less you charge in interest, the more attractive it is to borrow from you and do more deals. The idea is to make doing business irresistible.

LUCA: I see that, but this is a risky environment. If I don't charge them a good interest rate, I'm the one taking the risk.

SMILER: All due respect, boss, that may be what it takes. Look at it this way. Things are slow right now, but if the captains borrow from you, put the money on the street, and get the crews working, that's good for us. It may even build some new business. And then we'll get the money back and more in taxes.

LUCA: Hmph.

The Federal Reserve is a bank. Just like a bank, or our mafia boss, it can lend money if it wants to. The Fed lends money at what's called the **discount window**. It's the same as a person walking up to a teller's window in a regular bank and getting money out, except that the rate is a lot cheaper for banks—they get a big discount. Usually the discount window rate is about 1 percent higher than the federal funds rate, so it's still very low.

WINDOW OF OPPORTUNITY ➤

U.S. banks have made great use of the discount window during moments of crisis.

On September 12, 2001, following the 9/11 terror attacks, lending to banks through the discount window leapt to about $46 billion, more than two hundred times the daily average for the previous month.

On October 29, 2008, following the collapse of Lehman Brothers, lending through the discount window soared to a peak of $111 billion.

Banks don't usually use the discount window. It's more expensive than federal funds, and the bank has to provide collateral, usually government bonds, to secure the loan. So a bank will only use the discount window in an emergency. An emergency could be a problem with the bank that makes it risky to other banks, with the result that they won't lend it any money. Or it could be that other banks are so spooked by a shock to the economy that they hoard money. Banks did exactly this in the wake of the terrorist attacks in 2001 and the collapse of Lehman Brothers in 2008. In the latter case, the Fed had to cut the discount window rate by half a percent to get the banks to borrow, just as our mob friends Crumbs and Smiler told their boss to do.

And what if that's not enough?

LUCA: Okay, boys, you know why you're here. Charlie Bones got nabbed last week, and you've read about the indictments on the Palucci family. I know things are hard, but that doesn't mean we can stop doing business. I need to get the guys working or we all suffer. So how can we get things rolling out there?

SMILER: Here's an idea, boss. All of the crews have got markers out: people owe them a lot of money. But nobody's paying up, which means the captains are out of spending cash.

CRUMBS: Yeah, boss. That crew on the West Side owes fifty grand to Calabrese's boys, and the guys in Jesuit Heights are into Torre for a hundred grand at least. There's a bunch of other outstanding collections out there, and the captains ain't gonna do business until they get that money.

SMILER: You could buy those markers from the captains, boss, put a little more cash in their

pockets. Do that and they'll put the money
to work, I guarantee it.

LUCA: You guarantee it? Like you practically guaranteed that my giving them money would work?
Anyway, if I take on those markers, what am I
supposed to do? Collect 'em myself?

CRUMBS: Why not? We can get some guys to collect the
interest payments, let the gangs know we'll be
expecting the principal in a few months when
things get flush again.

LUCA: That's fine, assuming they don't go out of business in the meantime. And once again, it puts
me on the hook!

The captains are all owed money by various business counterparties.
So they're just like banks that are owed money by homeowners or businesses. A loan is an **asset**: it represents payment at a future date. Just like
a bond or a loan that can be sold in a secondary market, so these loans
can be bought by a benign boss, or a central bank.

These kinds of loans are called **private sector assets**, because
they're loans that have been made to organizations in the private sector, as distinct from **government assets**, which are loans made to the
government—Treasury bonds, in other words. The Fed is part of the
government, of course, so it's happy to buy government assets—like a
chef who's quite happy to eat her own cooking. She knows what's gone
into the dish, after all, so she knows she's not going to get sick. But
private sector assets are something of an unknown quantity. Just like
mysterious street food, which looks great but can leave you doubled
over in the fetal position, so private sector assets, whether they be debts
from a gang or loans made to a car company, can quickly go toxic. After
all, companies that issue bonds and families that take out mortgages
go bust all the time, so it's no wonder banks and other institutions

consider those assets to be much riskier than bonds sold by the government. And risky assets are more difficult to sell. So it's not surprising that governments don't want to buy them.

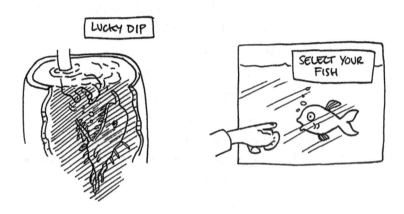

But sometimes they have to. If the Fed wants to get banks lending more to homeowners, the only way might be to buy mortgages from the banks, thereby freeing up that money for lending purposes. If the Fed wants the banks to lend to companies, it might buy corporate loans or bonds from them. If it wants to see more development loans, it might buy commercial real estate debt from the banks. By buying specific assets, the Fed can try to cajole the banks to lend more in those specific areas. But the Fed hates doing this, because if the homebuyers or the developers go bust, the Fed loses money—our money. Meanwhile the banks that sold the Fed the loans are laughing all the way to, well . . . the bank.

The economy has to be in pretty bad shape for the Fed to be buying these kinds of assets. But things have been exactly that bad: for the Japanese economy in the 1980s, and for the U.S. economy in the 2008–10 recession. In fact, they were worse, forcing the central banks to take another, very dangerous step: **printing money**.

Roll the Presses!

Up to now, the Fed has been dealing with a certain amount of money. Imagine America as a kiddie pool with a big water tank at one end. The tank is about a quarter full, and the pool is filled with just the right amount of water to keep the children happy. That tank is like the banking system, filled a quarter full with the cash that the banks are required to keep in reserve. The pool is like the economy, filled with just enough money to keep businesses humming and people employed.

There are two pipes in the bottom of the reserve tank. One pumps money into the economy, keeping the cash levels up. The other stops the cash levels from getting too high, as companies and individuals save their surplus money in the banking system. The Fed's job is to encourage the banks to pump in just enough money to the economy to keep it properly watered. It also wants to encourage savers to pump just enough money back into the banks to prevent the economy from becoming flooded with cash and drowning in cash—inflation, in other words.

But sometimes, when times are uncertain, the banks and the people don't play the Fed's game. The banks get worried that an economic drought is coming, so they hoard their money. They stop pumping. Meanwhile, people in the economy are also worried that they're going to run out of dough when the drought comes, so they want to get as much cash into the bank as fast as possible. So they pump even harder.

In a case like his, the drought is a self-fulfilling prophecy. There's no money going into the economy *from* the banks, and any money in the system is being pumped back *into* the banks. In our kiddie pool analogy, the tank is brimming with water. But the pool itself is almost bone dry. Which isn't much fun for the kids.

Up to this point in the story, the Fed has kept a certain amount of money circulating throughout the system. Just as our swimming pool is filled with a fixed amount of water that's pumped from the pool to the tank and back, so the set amount of money in the U.S. economy moves back and forth, from banks to consumers. If the Fed wants to restrict the amount of money in the system, it uses the repo system to take money out, like a caretaker pulling a bucket of water out of the tank and setting it aside. If the system needs more money the Fed uses the repo system to put money back in, like a caretaker pouring the bucket of water back into the tank. No extra money is added.

But when the system stops working, and all that money is stagnating in the banks rather than moving through the economy, the Fed has to resort to a drastic measure to jolt the system into action: it has to add more money. This is a dangerous thing to do, because in order to add more money, the Fed has to create *new* money. Some people use the technical term **quantitative easing** to describe this process: other people prefer the phrase **printing money**. Whatever you call it, the Fed hates doing it, be-

cause as we saw in earlier chapters, when there's too much money in the system, inflation rears its head, and it can wreak havoc on the economy.

This power to create money out of thin air is one of the greatest benefits to having a fiat currency. You'll remember from chapter 6 that when you have a fiat currency your dollar, pound, or yen is worth what it says on the note simply because the government says it's worth that much. "Trust us," the government says. "We'll make sure your dollar isn't worth any less tomorrow than what it is today." And people do trust, which makes it easy for a government to print money.

QE1 AND QE2 ➤

Japan was the first country to use quantitative easing, or QE, in 2001. But the biggest-ever example of quantitative easing took place in the United States, in the five years following the 2007 financial crisis. The Federal Reserve pumped $2.7 trillion of new money into the economy in two rounds of quantitative easing, called QE1 and QE2.

Once people trust you, you don't even have to make new banknotes. You can simply add a few zeros to a bank account. Which is exactly what the Fed does. It buys bonds from the banks, in just the same way as when it's controlling interest rates through open market operations. The difference is that in quantitative easing, it buys bonds to inject a certain quantity of *extra* money into the system. And in return for those bonds, rather than using money that's already in the system, it creates new money by crediting the bank's account. It's a bit like our kiddie pool caretaker sticking a hose into the water tank and turning on the tap, filling up the tank so high that the water *has* to start flowing into the pool. The caretaker has to find the water from somewhere: the Fed, on the other hand, is conjuring that money out of thin air. "We're good for it," the Fed says. "Trust us."

The idea of being able to create money so easily sounds quite tempting, doesn't it? Over the years, many government leaders have succumbed to the lure of the money printing press. Some have minted cash for selfish reasons, to enrich themselves and their cronies; some have set the presses running to pay for wars and other adventures; some have printed money with the more noble motive of trying to rescue their economies from recession. Whatever the reason, there's a real risk that printing money will devalue a currency and cause inflation. Fortunately, the Federal Reserve can destroy that new money as easily as it created it.

The Fed used quantitative easing to conjure $2.7 trillion out of thin air between 2007 and 2011. It did this by buying buckets of bonds and other debt from its prime dealer banks. That left the banks flush with extra cash in the form of bigger numbers in their accounts at the Federal Reserve. The Fed, meanwhile, was left loaded down with bonds that it really didn't need or want.

We noted earlier that when the Fed buys bonds from its prime dealers in open market operations, it attaches repurchase agreements to the transactions. It does exactly the same thing when it's using quantitative easing to inject extra cash into the system. Those repos help the Fed move money out of the economy and into the banking system when it feels there's too much cash sloshing around. Those repos also allow the Fed to dispose of the excess money that it's created.

Imagine that, at the peak of the financial crisis of 2008, the Federal Reserve created $10 billion by buying $10 billion worth of bonds from its primary dealer JT Gorgon. Now the economy is back in balance, and the Fed is worried about inflation. It wants to take some money out of the system, so it decides to destroy $10 billion. It calls up Gorgon and triggers the repo on that $10 billion bond purchase.

Remember, JT Gorgon was paid through its account at the Fed. The Fed received the bonds and credited the Gorgon account with $10 billion. The repo sends the bonds back to Gorgon, and the Fed now has a choice. It can either withdraw the $10 billion from the Gorgon account and transfer it elsewhere, keeping the money in the system, or it can delete it. The chairman of the Fed hits the delete key, and just like that, the money is destroyed.

It's a simple accounting entry, one that families replicate all the time. Families like the three little pigs, who by now are all working for Cuthbert's home renovation business.

CUTHBERT: Hey, Grub, I saw a guitar on sale today. It's only $200, down from $500. You should buy it.

GRUB: Yeah, I saw the sale. But I only have $150, and you don't pay us until the end of next week, remember.

CUTHBERT: Didn't you lend Dibble $50 last week? Can't he pay you back?

GRUB: Nah, he's broke. As usual. He spent it all on that trip to Atlantic City.

CUTHBERT: Did you at least make him write an IOU?

GRUB: Yeah. Not that it's worth the paper it's written on.

CUTHBERT: Okay, hand over that IOU, and I'll tell the bank to credit your account $50. But only if you agree to buy back that IOU for $50 any time I ask.

GRUB: Cool! Thanks, bro!

So far, so normal. Cuthbert has made it easier for his brother to make a sound investment in his budding musical career, and Grub uses the money to buy a guitar, just as Cuthbert intended. Everyone's happy. Until the following weekend.

CUTHBERT: Hey, where are you going all dressed up?

GRUB: Dibble's taking me clubbing.

CUTHBERT: Clubbing? Shouldn't you be practicing? I don't like you wasting your time and my money on nightclubs.

GRUB: Hey, it's my pay! I should be able to spend it any way I like.

CUTHBERT: Fair enough. You can party away *your* money if you want. But I want *my* money back.

GRUB: Whaddya mean *your* money?

CUTHBERT: I mean the fifty bucks I gave you in return for Dibble's IOU. You agreed to buy that IOU back anytime I wanted. And that time has arrived, my friend, so hand over my fifty.

GRUB: But I need the fifty! It'll be months before Dibble pays me back. If he ever does. Can I give you something else for it?

CUTHBERT: Nope. Our deal is done. Your pay is fifty bucks a month. No more, no less. Now hand over the cash.

As far as Grub is concerned, that $50 has been destroyed. Cuthbert may as well pull out his Zippo and burn up the note. The only way Grub is going to see any more excess money from his big brother is if Luca decides to buy another one of the IOUs that the feckless Dibble tosses about like confetti.

Cuthbert decided to use quantitative easing in Grub's finances because he wanted to achieve a certain goal. He wanted his brother to spend a certain quantity of money in a specific way. Likewise, the Fed injects a certain quantity of extra money into the banks to achieve a certain aim: to ease the lending logjam by making loans less risky for banks and cheaper for borrowers. But just as Cuthbert found that the excess money was encouraging unwelcome behavior in his brother, so the Fed might find that excess cash in the banking system can encourage unwelcome effects in the economy. Namely, inflation.

The repo system and the Fed's ability to create and destroy money are powerful tools, but all of these monetary policy devices are less like a surgeon's scalpel and more like an enforcer's blunt instrument. The Fed lends money and moves cash in and out of the banks' accounts with certain goals in mind, but there's no guarantee that the banks will do what the Fed wants. In the case of Cuthbert and his little brother, if Grub had decided not to buy a guitar, and went and spent his money on concert tickets instead, there's nothing Cuthbert could have done. Something like that happened in the U.S. banking system after the Federal Reserve completed QE1—its first round of quantitative easing. The banks were stuffed with excess cash, but rather than lending it out, as the Fed had intended, they sat on the money, hoarding it in their reserve accounts and using it to make their own balance sheets look healthier. QE1 had failed, which was why the Fed was forced to do a second round of quantitative easing, eventually pumping nearly $3 trillion of excess money into the U.S. financial system.

The government and the Fed were frustrated by their inability to get the banking system to behave the way they wanted. It was a clear example of the limits of the Fed's powers. But most people see that as a good thing. The banks' ability to operate independently and thus take the edge off the Federal Reserve's control is a natural counterbalance to the government's influence. Like so many other parts of the American system of government, the checks and balances built into the banking system ensure that power is shared between the public and the private sector. It's a system that works quite well when times are good, but it means the central bank can't do much to correct a faltering economy unless it has the full cooperation of its partners—the banks. And when an economy is failing, banks are likely to look out for their own interests before they worry about anyone else's.

NAME DROP ➤

. . . people just don't understand TARP and TALF and all these different toxic assets and purchase and repurchase and so on and so forth. They just don't understand it. When you try to explain it, when Chairman Bernanke tries to explain it, members of Congress try and explain it, it's Greek. It's no language. It doesn't—it's not understandable.

Senator Max Baucus (D-MT), congressional hearing on the economic crisis, March 4, 2009

The Fed's problem is further complicated by the fact that many of the organizations that lend money to consumers and companies today aren't banks at all. They're a collection of entities with odd names, such as conduits, Special Investment Vehicles, Special Purpose Vehicles, hedge funds, and Collateralized Debt Obligations. The Fed has no control over these strange financial creatures, which are barely understood by most people, and in many cases aren't regulated by any government organization at all. If you think this sounds shady, you're not alone; many politicians, regulators, and financial professionals think these entities are dodgy, perhaps even dangerous. So they've given these denizens of the financial underbelly a fitting collective name: the shadow banking system.

CHAPTER NINE

Gimme, Gimme, Gimme

Consumer Debt, Securitization, and Shadow Banking

There's an old saying that two emotions rule the economy and the markets: fear and greed. In bad times, fear rules. Most people are reluctant to take risks. They put off hiring new people, stop buying new things, steer clear of making new investments, and squirrel away any spare cash.

In good times, greed rules. People see how well their neighbors are doing and they want a piece of the good life for themselves. So they go shopping. But to actually do any buying, they need cash, and if they're not making that cash themselves, they need to borrow. Fortunately for the aspirational among us, we've developed an entire lending industry to satisfy our material desires. Today we can get a loan for almost anything. Credit cards help us to buy clothes and food, but there are also special loans to help us buy a college education, a car, a boat, or a home. And it doesn't stop with people. Companies are always looking for ways to offer us more stuff. To make all the things people want to buy, and to open all the stores to sell all that stuff, companies need to borrow, too—and there are a variety of borrowing options available to them.

Fifty years ago, if you were a consumer and you wanted to buy something expensive, like a train set or a helicopter, you went to a bank. But banking was a tough business back then. Risky, for one thing: the borrower might not pay you back! And competitive: so many other lenders out there, keeping interest rates down! Not to mention the regulations: all that red tape aimed at keeping customer money safe! It ain't easy making money by just taking deposits and making loans—not big money, anyhow.

And in the 1980s, banks wanted big money. The kind of big money that the investment banks were making with all their fee-based business. Commercial banks began asking themselves how they could get their hands on that fee money, without taking on risk. Interest income is great but it comes with an ever-present risk that the borrower might default. The fee that a borrower pays on first signing for a loan, on the other hand, comes without any risk. So one way lenders can make more money is to extend loans to borrowers, collect the fees, and then sell the loans to a **third party**, someone who's neither the borrower nor the lender. The risk of default is now assumed by the new owner of the loan, and the original lender simply pockets the fee and walks away.

Another way is to find a third party to *guarantee* the loan. For example, when Luca's son goes to buy a car, the financing company might lend him the money, but only on the understanding that Luca will guarantee that the interest payments will be made, and the debt eventually repaid.

The U.S. government institutionalized this loan guarantee process when it created the Federal Housing Administration in 1934. The government back then was looking for a way to stimulate an economy that was still struggling through the Great Depression. Housing seemed like a good target: when people buy houses, they usually spend more on the stuff that needs to go in their homes, too. That spending activity can rejuvenate a variety of other industries, from roofers to refrigerator makers. But it was tough for a homebuyer to get a mortgage. Loans were expensive, and banks were worried about taking risks.

The year 1934, an office in Washington, D.C. Jonas, a banker, has been invited to a meeting with Harry, a senator.

HARRY THE SENATOR:	Thanks for coming down from New York, Jonas.
JONAS THE BANKER:	No problem, Harry. I'm sure you'll make it worth my while. So whaddya need? Another campaign contribution?
HARRY:	We'll talk about that later. What I need from you, and from all you Wall Street guys, is for you to make more loans.
JONAS:	Companies aren't really borrowing that much right now, Harry.
HARRY:	I'm not talking about companies. I want you to lend to people, everyday Americans, so that they can buy homes.

JONAS: Yeah, right. So that they can default on their payments and walk away? No, thanks, Harry. We both know the American consumer is way too risky a bet right now. Find some other sucker to take the weight.

HARRY: How about if we guarantee the loans.

JONAS: Whaddya mean guarantee?

HARRY: I mean we'll commit to insuring the loans so that if the borrowers default, we'll pay you.

JONAS: Really? Just like that?

HARRY: Just like that. We're going to create an organization called the Federal Housing Administration. It will insure home loans so that you lenders don't end up on the hook.

JONAS: So I make the loan and hold it on my books, but if it goes bad then the government takes the hit?

HARRY: That's the size of it.

JONAS: And I collect the up-front fees and all the interest for as long as the loan is current?

HARRY: Yup.

JONAS: Well, now. What do you want in return?

HARRY: I just want you to lend FHA loans, Jonas. Nothing more.

JONAS: Well, then, Senator, I guess you have a deal!

The move worked. Home ownership rose, but not as much as the government wanted. The problem was that while the FHA loans were guaranteed, they were still counted on the banks' books, which meant the banks had to hold reserves against them. The government wanted to encourage more home ownership, and thus more borrowing, so in 1938 it came up with a new idea, called the Federal National Mortgage Association, or **Fannie Mae.**

The same two men meet, this time in New York

JONAS: Things must be pretty bad if you're making the trip up here, Senator. What's the rumpus?

HARRY: Well, Jonas, I need you Wall Street guys to make more loans.

JONAS: More loans? There's only so many we can handle, you know!

HARRY: Well, how about if you were able to make a bunch of loans, then sell them on immediately. Would you be able to make more loans then?

JONAS: Well sure, Harry, but there's no one buying FHA loans in the secondary market. Not in the kind of numbers you're looking for.

HARRY: What if the federal government bought them?

JONAS: The government? You're joking!

HARRY: Never been more serious. We're going to create a new organization. The Federal National Mortgage Association. It will buy any FHA loan made by any bank.

JONAS: Seriously? You're telling me it's going to buy every mortgage that I lend?

HARRY: Every FHA mortgage, yes.

JONAS: Hmm. So I'll lose the interest income. That's not good. But can I keep the fees?

HARRY: Sure.

JONAS: What's the catch?

HARRY: No catch. You just have to keep lending FHA loans.

JONAS: Sounds good to me, Harry. Now, have a cigar!

Fannie Mae's ability to buy huge amounts of mortgages guaranteed by the FHA and later by the Veterans Administration—today the Department of Veterans Affairs—meant that banks were able to lend as much as the American people desired. The government guarantee meant the loans came with low interest rates, which meant there was plenty of demand from consumers. Banks loved the business, which allowed them to **originate** loans for a fee and then sell them off immediately to Fannie Mae.

Fannie Mae was also good for the government, which watched happily as the rate of home ownership climbed steadily. But there was a complication. Fannie Mae was essentially a government department, which meant all the loans that it bought showed up as a big red mark on the federal budget. So, in 1968 the government made Fannie a public company (making sure that it kept a substantial investment, of course), which shifted all the debt off the federal balance sheet. Two years later the government created a sister (or brother) company for Fannie, called the **Federal Home Loan Mortgage Corporation**, or **Freddie Mac**. Freddie was also a public company, and again the government kept a big stake in the firm. The idea was to give Fannie some competition in the mortgage market, which would keep interest rates down.

The government didn't want to get out of the loan guarantee business altogether. It was worried that if something happened to Fannie and Freddie, there'd be no more support for the mortgage market. So when it made Fannie public, it also created the **Government National Mortgage Association**. **Ginnie Mae** focused entirely on supporting VA and FHA loans, as well as Farmers Home Administration loans. But Ginnie Mae used a different method to support the mortgage market. Instead of simply buying and selling mortgages, as Fannie did, the folks at Ginnie came up with something called **securitization**.

> **GINNIE:** Good morning, JT. Thank you for coming all the way down from Wall Street today.
>
> **JT GORGON:** This better be worth the trip, Ginnie.

GINNIE: Relax, JT. I think you're going to like this. Now, I heard you lent a thousand mortgages last month. I want you to hold on to them.

JT GORGON: What? Those mortgages are worth twenty million bucks! What about our deal to sell them to Fannie Mae?

GINNIE: We're trying something different. Instead of selling them, I want you to pool those mortgages in a separate trust. Every month that pool is going to generate a big chunk of cash, as the borrowers make their interest payments.

JT GORGON: Yeah. So what?

GINNIE: So that trust looks a lot like a regular company now. A shoe company, for example, buys leather and rubber, makes shoes, and then sells them for a profit. Raw materials in one end, cash out the other. This trust is exactly the same, except that the raw materials are mortgages. Mortgages in one end, cash out the other.

JT GORGON: Except that a regular company has investors, which lend it the money it needs to buy its raw materials. Right now, I'm the only investor in this trust, and I can't afford to buy that many mortgages!

GINNIE: I know, which is why I want you to go out and find people to invest in the trust. Let *them* lend the trust the $20 million, which funds the purchase of VA and other mortgages from you. In return the trust sells the investors a bond, and any interest and principal paid is passed through the trust to them.

JT GORGON: Let me get this right. I create a trust, which recruits a bunch of investors. The investors lend the trust $20 million. The trust then buys $20 million of mortgages from me. It then issues bonds to the investors and pays those bonds with the interest from the mortgages.

GINNIE: That's it.

JT GORGON: Well, that would work for me. I'd get the fees from lending the mortgages, and selling the mortgages to the trust would get the loans off my books. But the trust won't work. No investor's going to buy those bonds. If people get into trouble and stop paying interest on the mortgages, or if they pay off their mortgages early, the trust won't be able to pay the interest to the bondholders.

GINNIE: That's where I come in. I'll guarantee the bonds. Even if every borrower in the pool goes bust; even if they all prepay their mortgages, I'll commit to making those interest payments for as long as the bond is current.

JT GORGON: I like it! Your guarantee will allow the trust to keep operating, no matter what. Which means investors will keep buying the bonds, and I can keep selling mortgages to the trustees. You're a genius, Ginnie! What are you calling this thing?

GINNIE: Well, the wonks figured that because these trusts will be selling bonds, which are a security, we could call it a securitization.

JT GORGON: Hmm. Securitization. It's a bit of a mouthful, but I like how it makes the whole business sound very mysterious. Count me in.

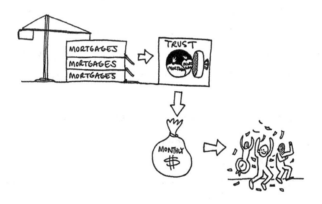

The first mortgage-backed security was created in 1970. It was called a **pass-through**, because the interest and principal on all the loans in the pool were simply passed straight through to the bondholders (after the people running the trust were paid a fee, of course). Freddie Mac was the first to catch on to the idea, and created its first pass-through MBS in 1971. Fannie Mae took a while longer, only debuting the technique in 1981.

Securitization was a boon for homeowners, for the government, and for the banks who lent these mortgages. But investors weren't quite so happy.

JT Gorgon:	JT Gorgon for Mr. Lizzarde.
Receptionist:	Connecting you now, sir.
Lizzarde:	Whaddya want, JT? I already told your boy I'm

not buying any of your measly pass-through securities.

JT Gorgon: Jimmy, I—

Lizzarde: There's no return on those things. I can make
more money playing poker with my kids. Come
and talk to me when you can offer me a bond
with a decent interest rate.

Pass-through mortgage-backed securities simply weren't profitable
enough for many investors. The guarantee on the bonds made MBS very
low-risk, but low risk also means low reward. Aggressive investors who
wanted to earn a lot of money on their investments simply couldn't do it
in the mortgage market. So they turned up their noses at MBS. And that
got the smart men and women on Wall Street thinking.

JT Gorgon: How about if we create a securitization using private mortgages?

Lizzarde: No government guarantees?

JT Gorgon: Nope. Not on the mortgages, and not on the
bonds, either.

Lizzarde: There's no way you can make that work. Some
of the borrowers are certain to prepay their
mortgages. And some are certain to default.
Without the guarantee on the mortgages, you're
going to have less money to pay the investors.
That would be okay if the bonds were guaranteed, but they're not. That's a huge risk for investors like me. I'm gonna want a huge interest
rate to compensate me for taking that risk. You
simply can't afford to pay me and all the others
all that much each month.

JT Gorgon: How about if I pay you even more?

LIZZARDE: Don't be ridiculous! I've just told you it can't be done. But I'm listening.

JT GORGON: How about if I let investors take different levels of risk? You take a big risk, you get a bigger-than-average interest payment. You take a small risk, you get a smaller-than-average payment. It'd be just like buying bonds in General Electric.

It was a natural next step for Wall Street. In her conversation with JT, Ginnie compared the MBS mortgage pool to a company. Both got money from investors and both paid the investors back with the profits they made. But as JT pointed out to Lizzarde, many companies have more than one class of investor. As we saw in chapter 3, many companies have *multiple* levels of investors. The senior lenders at the top of the ladder lend for a shorter period and get paid first, so they take little risk and get paid least in return. The next class of bondholders lends for a little longer and is second in line to get paid each month. For that extra risk, those bondholders get paid a little more. And so on and on down the ladder, each class of investor lending for a longer term, taking a little more risk, and being paid a little more interest as compensation.

As JT pointed out, why not treat a pool of mortgages the same way?

Two investment banks, Salomon Brothers and First Boston, teamed up to give the idea a try. In 1983, they created a new securitization for Freddie Mac that offered a range of bonds based on a pool of private mortgages. Each class of bond had a different tenor and a different interest rate. Just like in a corporation, the safest, shortest-duration investments were at the top and the riskiest and longest were at the bottom. It was a mortgage-backed security with a twist, so it needed a new name. They called it a **collateralized mortgage obligation**.

It might help to think about a collateralized mortgage obligation as a pyramid of glasses, piled up in several tiers on a silver tray. Each tier represents a class of investor, the senior bondholders at the top, then the

mid-level or **mezzanine** bondholders in the middle, and the junior bond-holders at the bottom. The tray is where the equity holders stand.

Now we pop the bottle of champagne. The bottle is the bundle of mort-gages. At the end of the month, all the mortgage borrowers make their interest payments and the cash flows, like champagne pouring out of the bottle. It flows out over the pyramid, filling the top tier of bondholders first, then the mezzanine tier, then the bottom and finally it fills the silver tray. And the same thing happens month after month after month.

If some of the mortgage borrowers get into trouble and fail to make their interest payments, or if they prepay or refinance their mortgages, less money will spout out of the mortgage pool and cascade over the

pyramid. The top tier will likely still be filled, so those bondholders get paid, and maybe the mezzanine, too. But the chances of the bottom-tier lenders and the equity investors being left dry become very real. That's why the junior bondholders get the biggest interest payments, while the payouts to the senior lenders are the smallest.

The collateralized mortgage obligation was a stroke of genius. It created a range of risk profiles and investment durations, and thereby appealed to many more investors. Now conservative banks could buy bonds that gave them a small, steady, and all-but-certain income, while speculators could gamble big with their bond investments, hoping for a fat payout each month.

And just like that, the genie was out of the bottle. Lenders realized that anything that generated cash flow or a steady stream of money each month could be securitized. Whether it was a mortgage, an aircraft lease, a student loan, or a book royalty payment, if it had cash flow, it was called an asset, which meant it could be turned into a so-called **asset-backed security**, or **ABS**. In 1985 Marine Midland Bank created a securitization of car loans. The following year, Bank One securitized a pool of credit card receivables. Pretty soon, banks were filling these so-called securitiza-

tion **vehicles** with corporate bonds and loans, notably those loans made as part of leveraged buyouts.

Whether the collateral in these asset-backed securities was personal credit card receivables or corporate loans, securitization did several things all at the same time.

It gave investors easy access to a wide variety of areas of finance. Now a single investor could put money into mortgages, credit cards, and car loans, rather than focusing on just one area. Investors liked the idea of being able to diversify this way, so they asked for more of these types of bonds.

That demand in turn fueled demand for more car loans, mortgages, and credit cards to put into the securitizations, which meant banks were pressured into going out and making more loans.

Suddenly it became a lot easier to get a loan. And that was great news for the economy. At the consumer level, it gave individuals access to money to buy goods and services in volumes that businesses had never seen before. That income allowed those businesses to grow, to hire more people, who in turn consumed more. At the corporate level, it gave companies access to the kind of money that gave them the freedom to do the kinds of things that companies could only have dreamed of in the past. Now they could expand into other parts of the globe, create new markets for their goods, even buy out their competitors.

We noted earlier that banks have to keep a certain amount of money in reserve for every loan they hold on their books, which in the past limited the number of loans they could make. Banks are also very cautious about whom they lend money to—if they are holding on to the loan. If a borrower defaults on a loan, the bank loses money, so banks tended in the past only to lend money to people who were highly likely to pay them back. But the proliferation of asset-backed securities meant that banks could now offload every loan they made. The banks collected a fee for making the loan, and in many cases they also made arrangements to collect the loan's interest payments—for another fee, of course. But they didn't have to hold the loans on their accounts. Not only did that free up billions of dollars that they could lend out, but it also meant they didn't have to worry quite so much about the possibility that the borrower might fail to pay any interest on the loan.

In the late 1990s and early 2000s, the banks were happy, because they were making lots of fee money without taking much of a long-term risk. American consumers and companies were happy because more money in the system and the banks' dwindling concern about credit quality made it easier for them to borrow. But investors were happiest of all. Asset-backed securities, whether they were based on mortgages, corporate bonds, or student loans, were enormously profitable. America was growing rapidly, unemployment was falling, and incomes were rising. Investors noticed that most people were making their interest payments, and the **default rate** of companies and individuals was way, way down. Many figured the

riskiest bonds sold by an asset-backed security were less risky than they seemed. So they demanded more.

And the lenders were happy to oblige. As the 1990s wore on, they doled out mortgages, car loans, and credit cards to people who would never have qualified for a loan twenty years before. Those borrowers often paid painfully high interest rates on their loans, which reflected the possibility that they wouldn't be able to make their payments. But the investors who bought bonds backed by bundles of mortgages or car loans

didn't mind: the more the borrowers had to pay, the higher the interest payments went on the bonds, and the more cash went into their pockets.

Financiers have a kind of code for describing certain types of borrowers. People who are likely to pay the interest on their loans, and pay the loans back, are called **prime borrowers**. Does that make them sound like a piece of meat? Well, if you've ever bought a piece of steak, you'll know that prime cuts of meat come with a great deal of marbling. This means they have plenty of fat, which makes the steak juicy and easy to cut and eat when it's cooked. Borrowers are the same. The "fatter" or wealthier they are, the easier they are to deal with. Prime borrowers make their payments regularly and they pay their principal. Even when times are hard, they have money in reserve that they can use to keep paying, or **stay current** on their debt. In a banker's eyes, prime borrowers are as juicy and delicious as a piece of prime steak. Borrowers who are lean, who have less or no cash in reserve, look a lot less tasty. A small upset can have a big effect on these lean borrowers' ability to stay current. The leanest borrowers of all, the ones that are least likely to stay current on their debts, are called **subprime borrowers**.

In the early 2000s, an unprecedented amount of debt was being lent to subprime borrowers, who opened credit card accounts, bought cars, boats, and, of course, houses. We now know that many lenders were giving mortgages to people without asking for any collateral, or even proof of earnings. These mortgages were termed **subprime**, like the borrowers who were likely to fail to make their payments, and they were bundled up into securitization vehicles just like all the rest of the debt that was out there. The lenders didn't care about the borrowers, because they could simply sell the mortgages on to a securitization trust. If the borrower defaulted, it was no longer the lender's problem.

The trusts didn't think it was their problem, either. The economy was booming, so that enough subprime borrowers were making their payments to funnel money to most of the investors who bought the bonds in these securitization vehicles. Most of the glasses in the pyramid were filling up, as it were. These bonds did so well that some enterprising financiers decided to take those bonds and securitize them, too! They called these new vehicles collateralized debt obligations, or **CDOs**, and they marketed them as completely safe.

Good financiers rarely take what another financier says about a certain investment at face value; they certainly don't believe that anything is completely safe. Good financiers do what's called **due diligence**, which means they pop the hood on an investment, whether it's a company or a collection of loans, they poke around in the guts of the thing, and they make sure that they're not getting involved in anything too risky. But due diligence is hard work, and in the past many financiers have proven too busy, or maybe too lazy, to do that work. Instead, they've relied on **ratings**.

CREDIT WHERE IT'S DUE ➤

On October 31, 2007, a stock analyst named Meredith Whitney shocked the banking world with a report that said Citigroup, one of the biggest banks in the nation, had too many bad home loans and was barely making enough money to operate.

The statement seemed absurd. Citi was the recipient of stamps of approval from analysts at all three **ratings agencies** and the best investment banks. The bank insisted it had plenty of money and that Whitney was plain wrong.

But Whitney was right. She had ignored her peers, dug deep into Citi's balance sheet, and gone through its operations with a clear, hard eye. Other analysts rushed to do their own due diligence a little more diligently. Many downgraded Citi, and a week later, the bank's CEO resigned.

Ratings agencies are private organizations that study a company's balance sheet and make a pronouncement on the company's performance. Companies don't have to be rated, but if they aren't, it's a lot more difficult to find investors. It's a bit like working for an investment banker. You don't have to have an MBA, but it's a heck of a lot harder to get a job if you don't. And just like recruiters, who use a candidate's qualifications as a guide but interview carefully before hiring, so smart investors use a company's rating as a guide but do their own research before putting any money into it.

Ratings are like academic qualifications in another way. Just as a student pays the university for her degree, so companies pay ratings agencies for their ratings. And just like in the college system where universities compete to get students in the door, there's furious competition among ratings agencies to rate America's corporations. Except that there are just three official ratings agencies—Fitch Ratings, Moody's Investors Service, and Standard

& Poor's—so the competition is intense. There's a danger that an agency might be tempted to offer a company a more lenient grade in return for that company's business. And that a company might be tempted to shop around between the three agencies, looking for the most favorable rating.

This shopping around is called **ratings arbitrage**, and it occurred a lot in the securitization world during the early 2000s. Some of the organizations that created asset-backed securities, including CMOs and CDOs, used ratings arbitrage to get the best ratings on their CDO bonds. Sometimes the ratings agencies succumbed and gave CDOs favorable ratings. At other times they made big, incorrect assumptions about how those CDOs were structured, and how they would perform. And many investors trusted them blindly.

It wasn't long before the banks were surpassed as the chief stokers of the engine of economic growth. Previously it had been demand from a bank's investors that motivated the bank to lend. Now it was investors in securitization vehicles that were making all the demands. The government monitors banks quite carefully, with the result that most tend to be rather conservative. Most banks didn't feel comfortable making the kind of risky loans that investors in asset-backed bonds wanted them to make. So a gap appeared in the market. And a new class of lenders stepped up in droves to fill it.

The Shadow Banking System

They called them the shadow banks. These banks didn't take deposits. They didn't make interest payments. They didn't have main street branches. Many of them didn't even have physical addresses, or even phone numbers. Some had vaguely familiar names, such as investment bank, money-market fund, or hedge fund, but others adopted outlandish monikers like Structured Investment Vehicle or conduit. They were only "banks" in the sense that they acted as intermediaries between investors who wanted to reap the huge returns promised by these new moneymaking vehicles, and people who wanted to borrow money from anyone who would lend it to them.

> Colleagues call it the "shadow banking system" because it has lain hidden for years, untouched by regulation yet free to magically and mystically create and then package subprime loans in [ways] that only Wall Street wizards could explain.
>
> **Bill Gross, head of the investment company Pimco**

By 2007 the shadow banking system was responsible for more than $10 trillion in loans, more than half the debt generated by the entire U.S. financial system. And yet, even though the shadow banks dominated banking, they operated out of sight of most Americans and much of the government, too. There were great advantages to operating unnoticed by the public. It meant no interference from customers, no complaining phone calls, and no snooping by the press. There were even greater benefits to being unobserved by the government. The system of oversight that monitored the banks and kept them in line had been slowly rolled

back over the years, and regulators simply hadn't kept up with developments in the banking business. Even though the new class of lenders had grown bigger than the banks, they operated almost entirely outside the regulatory framework. In 2007, every bank in America was required to report to a regulator, and some reported to several. Yet most of the new breed of lenders, responsible for half the loans made in the country, didn't report to anyone at all.

Even if the press and the politicians had an inkling of what was going on in the shadowy alleyways of Wall Street, they said nothing about it. Debt was the engine of the massive boom in the economy from 2002 onward, and the shadow banking system was the grimy stoker shoveling the fuel. Everyone benefited from debt: the people from all walks of life who could buy huge houses and max out their credit cards filling those houses up with flat-screen TVs and leather recliners; the companies who could set up operations in far-flung corners of the world one day and then gobble up a neighbor the next; the investors who rode the soaring stock market, and used asset-backed securities to turn a billion dollars into a hundred billion on paper in less than a year; the politicians who could point to the buildings rising in their districts and the unemployment numbers falling all over the nation; the president who could boast about the country's stunning growth rate and announce the forces of terror had failed to suppress the American way of life.

Occasionally some egghead would try to spoil the party by muttering darkly about the overextension of credit, or the lack of regulation in the banking sector, or the dangerous and poorly understood interconnectedness of the financial system. But most Americans had no idea what the eggheads were burbling about. And most of those who did understand the warnings dismissed them, saying they didn't acknowledge the benefits of a truly free and unregulated market.

Unfortunately, however, the eggheads were right. Debt, and consumer debt in particular, was the fuel that the stokers of the financial industry shoveled into the engine of the 1990–2007 economic boom. The trouble with fuel is that someone has to pay for it. A borrower can play the game of paying one loan off with another for so long, but one day the bill comes due and the debt must finally be paid. And in 2007, the bills starting coming due, all over America.

CHAPTER TEN

Architects of Our Own Destruction

Decline and Recovery in the Financial Markets

I t seems obvious now that the U.S. financial markets were headed for disaster in the run-up to the 2008 financial crisis. All the ingredients were in place: too much borrowing by people who were unlikely to pay the money back; light or nonexistent regulation of every player in the financial system; incompetence in the ratings agencies; ignorance on Capitol Hill; possible fraud and corruption in the mortgage departments of lenders; gullibility in the boardrooms of investment funds all over the world; and hubris at the headquarters of banks, investment banks, fund trustees, and consumers, a great many of whom were consumed by greed and convinced that they would be able to lend and borrow forever.

Boom and Bust, Ad Infinitum

Not that any of this was new. In fact, to historians of financial crashes, it all looked very familiar. One or more of these ingredients featured in the mix of every collapse of the markets going back to the South Sea Bubble in 1720. Back then, it was fraudulent manipulation of shares, corruption in the government, and irrational hubris that brought the British financial system crashing down. In 1819, overborrowing by America to finance a war triggered a slew of bank failures and a market crash. In 1825, a lack of due diligence by investors in Latin American companies—including some fictitious firms—tore down the British financial system. Mayhem in the markets occurred roughly every ten years on either side of the Atlantic until the granddaddy of meltdowns, the Wall Street Crash of 1929.

BUBBLICIOUS ➤

Market crashes are usually the direct result of a bubble popping. A bubble occurs simply when the price of something rises far higher than what the thing is really worth. Eventually people catch on, and stop buying, and the bubble bursts.

In Holland, between November 1636 and February 1, 1937, a mania for tulip bulbs pushed prices to 5,000 guilders from about 50. A few weeks later, the price plummeted back to earth, leaving many Hollanders penniless.

During the dot-com bubble of the late 1990s, investors raced to buy into companies that were making no money and had no workable business plan. One company, named boo.com, raised $160 million in 1998 and 1999. The investors lost every cent of their money in May 2000, when the company went bust.

Housing prices soared in Nevada, Florida, California, and other parts of the United States in the mid-2000s as Americans rushed to buy real estate. Some bought multiple homes, often without ever even seeing them, and prices more than doubled in many areas. When reality sank in around 2007, prices went into free fall, and the stock market soon followed.

Just like the run-up to the 2008 financial crisis, the decade before the 1929 crash was one long boom. In the 1920s, investors, which included ordinary Americans, borrowed large amounts of money to buy shares in the stock market. Banks funneled depositor money into stocks, too, and the market ratcheted higher, year after year until, on October 24, 1929, it crashed and lost 11 percent of its value in a single day. Two years later, the market had lost nearly 90 percent of its value.

Overborrowing, slack regulation, incompetence and ignorance, hubris and greed led to the crash. The financial system was so destabilized that a series of bank panics followed, cutting off access to credit and paving the way for the Great Depression. But while the fallout from the 1929 crash laid waste to America's financial landscape, it also prepared the ground for the construction of a new regulatory regime. The government was determined to protect the American people and their money. It passed the Securities Act of 1933 to ensure proper disclosure of information on stocks and bonds, and the Banking Act of 1933 to prevent banks from speculating with depositors' money, among other things. Other acts followed, erecting solid boundaries around the capital markets and the banking system.

It was a remarkably successful system, in terms of its ability to protect

American investors. Over the next fifty years, the markets had their ups and downs, but there was no great upset on the scale of the 1929 collapse until the late 1980s. By then, however, a great deal had changed. As we learned in chapter 6, technology had begun to take over from humans in the early 1980s, and a whole range of financial tasks was outsourced to computers.

The Rise of the Machines

In the commercial banking sector, banks used computers to move money around, which made it easier for them to make loans. In the securities trading sector, investment banks and trading firms recognized that computer technology made buying and selling stocks, bonds, and futures quick and easy, and therefore potentially much more profitable. Investors began pressing trading organizations to buy and sell more, and more quickly, and the move to computerization gathered pace.

Things went well at first; throughout the early 1980s the bond, stock, and futures markets experienced a surge in activity as institutions that adopted computers were able to initiate many more trades. But not every investment firm was a convert. A great number of investors still preferred the tangibility of a paper trail. Many of the companies that used computers to trigger the trades still used paper to close those transactions. So, while the front offices of the trading firms were doing a lot more business with their whizzy new machines, the inky-fingered clerks in the back

offices of institutions in London, New York, Frankfurt, and Tokyo were slowly becoming buried under the heaps of paper generated by all that buying and selling.

In banks and finance companies all over the world, technology advocates and skeptics debated the problem. Computer lovers argued technology was the solution to the growing logjam. Better, faster machines would make the system more efficient, they insisted. The technophobes fretted about security. Computers can be hacked, or they can break down, they warned. And then there was human error: all it takes is one **fat finger**—the phrase used to describe a faulty keystroke—to wipe out a billion dollars in the blink of an eye.

The technologists gradually began to win over even the most conservative of investment firms. On the one hand, banks and institutions needed a solution to the short-term paper jam that was beginning to hurt their businesses—and hiring more clerks was costly and time-consuming. On the other hand, they were persuaded that computers would make the markets even more efficient in the long term, which could help them make pots more money. The twin attractions of a speedy solution to a growing problem and the promise of more business down the line eclipsed bankers' concerns about the computers' vulnerability to hackers, fools, and techno-criminals. Checks and bonds and banknotes can also be forged, stolen, or lost, they rationalized; digital transactions would be easier to keep track of, and to audit.

Any waverers were brought into line by the events that followed October 27, 1986, the day the British government changed the rules governing the London exchanges. First, the government opened up the market to allow banks and foreign firms to trade. Second, it made London an electronic exchange.

The City, as London's financial center is called, operated a bit like a very exclusive gentleman's club in the 1980s. Only a handful of firms were allowed to trade securities, and all trading was done face-to-face. The new rules had the effect of driving an Abrams tank through the

club's mahogany doors, and letting the entire world storm in behind it. Now almost anyone could be a member of the club, and they didn't even need to occupy one of the plush leather chairs to do business there. All they needed was a license and a computer modem.

Financiers call the changes the **Big Bang**, because, like the Big Bang that created our universe, they didn't just transform the securities world, they created a new one. London instantly became the global financial capital as money poured into the City from all over the world, and banks and institutions made billions of trades on their new systems. But just as the original Big Bang must have destroyed what went before in order to create our universe, so London's Big Bang wrought havoc on the markets.

Behind the plush velvet curtain that shrouded the financial world in mystery, bankers and investors struggled to adjust to the new ways of doing business. Many banks and institutions were still playing catch-up, so there was still a paperwork bottleneck in much of the system. Moreover, the new computers occasionally became overwhelmed, to the point where they were unable to move quickly enough to match the buy and sell orders made by investors. In short, the bottleneck clogging the smooth operation of the markets was one step short of turning into gridlock.

Getting with the Program

Computers could trade infinitely faster than any human, so many invest-ment companies had devised programs that gave the machines instruc-tions when to buy and when to sell automatically. Starting in the 1980s, this so-called **program trading** effectively outsourced many human op-erations to the machines. For example, an investment manager holding five million General Motors shares might think the company's stock was worth between $9 and $15 per share. So she'd write a program instruct-ing the computer to sell if the stock rose to $15. And if it fell below $9? Well, that would signal something was badly wrong with the company, something she might not necessarily know about, so she'd want the com-puter to sell then, too.

And then she'd go and make a cup of tea.

Pretty smart, eh? Except that a program like that doesn't take the outlier into account. Say an investor suddenly decides he has to sell a big chunk of GM stock. Maybe he needs to meet a margin call, or a gambling debt, or make a mortgage payment on his castle in Scotland. So he sells at $8.99 a share. Or maybe the trade occurs because someone makes a mistake. Maybe someone has a fat finger! Whatever the reason for the trade, the computer doesn't care. It doesn't check the newswires, doesn't pick up the phone to see what's going on, doesn't turn on the TV. It simply does its job, according to the program written for it, and it sells five million GM shares.

Oops.

One trade doesn't usually make a great difference to the market. Un-less it's a really big trade. When millions of shares of a single stock are bought or sold, that can **move the market**, by driving the price of that stock up or down sharply. If our sale of five million GM shares pushes the stock price below other computers' program-generated thresholds, they'll start to sell, too, and the next thing you know, computers all over the world are selling their GM holdings. By the time our investment man-ager has sugared her tea, the stock is down to $7 and falling like a stone.

SELL!

SELL!

SELL!!

This kind of steep decline can have all sorts of ripple effects. Investors can program their computers to sell an entire portfolio of shares if the portfolio's value drops below a certain amount. If one investor is holding a large amount of GM, the decline in its stock price could cut the value of his portfolio in half and trigger a sale of every share he owns. Now there are a dozen shares tumbling, and suddenly the entire market is falling out of bed.

Something like this happened almost exactly a year after the Big Bang, on October 19, 1987. Traders called it **Black Monday**. To this day, no one knows for sure what triggered a wave of selling that started in Hong Kong on that Monday morning and swept across the globe. But the effects on every financial center were dramatic. Imagine stepping into an elevator on the 100th floor of a skyscraper to find the lift descending somewhat faster than usual. Rather nervous, you press the 80th floor button, but you're already passing 75. Seriously worried now, you stab the button marked 50. Too late again! Panicking, you pound one button after another, and eventually, you get out on the 20th floor, sweaty, shaken, and vowing you'll never set foot in an elevator again.

This happened in portfolios across the globe as exchanges in every financial center from Tokyo to New York were deluged with buy and sell orders from traders. Many companies hadn't upgraded completely to

computerization at that point, and the paper gridlock in the system pre-vented back offices from actually approving the trades quickly enough. In New York, many trades were executed more than one hour late. This meant that investors who thought they sold at one price discovered later that they had in fact sold at much lower levels. And they received a lot less money as a result.

Not everyone agrees that program trading caused the Black Monday crash, but in the immediate aftermath it was clear to everyone that there was no way to reverse the march of technology on the financial services industry. It was the kind of plot twist a science fiction writer would be proud of: the machines may have caused the problem, but they appeared to be the only solution. Bankers, investors, and regulators concluded the only option was to go all in, to abandon traditional face-to-face trading, handshakes, and paperwork, and adopt **electronic settlement**, where computers took over many the functions and responsibilities of human beings, in front office and back.

CHANGING THE GAME >

Remember the **low volume, high volatility** rule mentioned in chapter 1? That disappeared when the high-frequency traders arrived on the scene. These machines could zigzag around the market like crazy, and trade billions of shares at the same time. As I explained, a market is like a dance hall full of waltzing couples. Only with **high-frequency trading**, those couples are robots that can dance incredibly fast and close together, their sensors assuring they never collide with each other, or with the occasional human who has gathered up the courage to join them on the floor. High-frequency trading meant the markets were now operating at high volume, and exhibiting high volatility at the same time.

Electronic settlement and program trading were merely baby steps in the development of the computerized securities markets. By the mid-2000s, the computer programs governing the machines' activities had become complicated enough to warrant a technical name, **algorithms**. Program trading got a new name, too, **high-frequency trading**, and the companies that used this superfast computerized trading technique began to dominate the markets.

A glance at the graph of the Standard and Poor's index of the 500 largest publicly traded companies in the United States shows how the introduction of computer technology affected the markets. The S&P 500 had bumped along below the 100 mark since the index was created in 1957, but as technology took hold in the early 1980s, and investment companies were able to use computing power to trade exponentially more than they had in the past, the value of companies began to soar. As money flooded into the stock markets, the S&P 500 doubled between 1980 and 1986, then doubled again and again, roughly every six years until it hit 1520 in September 2000.

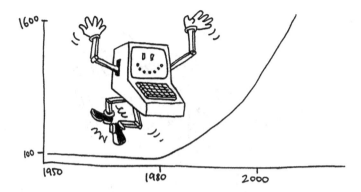

The stock markets weren't the only organizations that benefited from the advances in technology in the 1980s and beyond. The bond and futures markets exploded, too, and the number of **day traders** began to increase, as individuals rushed to get a piece of the action. These were ordinary Americans betting their own money on the movements of everything from stocks to interest rates, increasingly using computers as the technology improved. Corporations began setting up finance arms. For example, General Electric set up the forebear of General Electric Capital in 1983. And commercial banks, which had been barred from doing much in the stocks-and-bonds-buying business by the Securities Act of 1933, started lobbying for increased access to the markets.

BUY!

BUY!

BUY!!

The carefully crafted regulatory system set up after the Great Crash of 1929 was utterly besieged. Regulators appeared ill-equipped to keep pace with the technological developments in the markets, and many politicians felt little incentive to rein in the financial services that were doing so much good for the economy. Some in the government wondered to what heights the markets might soar if they were unencumbered by regulatory restrictions altogether. Encouraged by banks and lobby groups, politicians and regulators began dismantling the system. They relaxed barriers to commercial bank involvement in the securities trading business until, in 1999, the government repealed part of the Glass-Steagall Act and formally allowed securities firms, commercial banks, investment banks, and insurance companies to consolidate.

The repeal of the act was a formality because many banks were already doing plenty of securities business in the United States. Originally a commercial bank, J. P. Morgan & Company built up its investment banking business throughout the 1990s. Bank of America had run its own Banc of America Securities division for years, and bought the broker Robertson Stephens in 1997. Citicorp bought the Travelers Group, which included the Salomon Smith Barney brokerage, in 1997. Deutsche Bank bought the investment bank Bankers Trust in 1998. First Union bought Bowles Hollowell Connor & Company in the same year. In 1999, other banks rushed to catch up. Wachovia bought First Union. Chase Manhattan Bank went on a spree, buying the investment bank Hambrecht & Quist, the London merchant bank Flemings, and the Beacon investment bank.

Flush from the money they were making in the securities markets, a relatively small number of commercial and investment banks began to dominate the Wall Street skyline. For decades these banks had spent billions of dollars in Washington, D.C., persuading politicians to punch holes in the regulatory system that had kept them in check and protected ordinary American investors for more than fifty years. The money the banks spent bought them a vast amount of freedom. But that didn't mean they trusted each other.

It was quite the opposite: the banks didn't trust each other in the slightest. And they wanted to find a way to protect themselves. The regulatory system was of little use to them. It was designed to safeguard the consumer, not to protect banks from each other. So the banks began to build an informal security network, one that used insurance, rather than rules. The theory was that banks should be able to do any kind of business they wanted. If they screwed up, they would fail, but if they were smart, they would protect against mishaps by buying insurance.

And that's what they did. They bought insurance policies on bonds, mortgages, corporate loans, and CDOs. But they weren't like any insurance policy that ordinary Americans knew about, at least not in name. We talked about them in chapter 4. They were called **credit default swaps**, or CDSs.

The Ties That Bind

CDSs may have appeared like black magic to ordinary people, but they behaved in a similar fashion to the kind of insurance that Americans buy all the time. In a way, the banks were like a neighborhood of homeowners buying insurance for the house, the garage, the refrigerator, the kids, and all the rest of it. Imagine you're a homeowner and you go to an insurance company to buy a policy to protect your roof and your car. You also want to insure your dog from being run over and your freezer from thawing out, but the company won't do that for you. One day you're having a conversation with your neighbor.

> **TERRY:** Lovely day.
>
> **JUNE:** I s'pose.
>
> **TERRY:** Why so glum?
>
> **JUNE:** I want to insure my dog.
>
> **TERRY:** Your dog?
>
> **JUNE:** Yes. I'm worried he's going to get run over, but ABC Insurance won't insure him for me.
>
> **TERRY:** Well, he's a pretty smart dog. Well trained, too. And you keep him on a tight leash. Seems pretty low-risk to me. How much do you want to insure him for?
>
> **JUNE:** Five thousand dollars.
>
> **TERRY:** I could do that for you.
>
> **JUNE:** You?
>
> **TERRY:** Sure, why not? You pay me $5 a month, and I'll

insure your dog. If he gets run over anytime in the next five years, I'll pay you $5,000.

JUNE: Wow! Okay! Say, what are you doing with that chain saw?

TERRY: I'm worried the tree in my yard is gonna come down on my roof. It's a shame, because I love that tree, and the shade really helps with the AC bills. But the insurance company won't insure my roof against tree damage.

JUNE: That's a pretty healthy tree. And it's young, too. Plus we don't get that much wind here. How much damage do you want to insure against?

TERRY: Oh, about $10,000.

JUNE: Tell you what, if you pay me $10 a month, if that tree takes your roof down at any time in the next five years, I'll pay you ten grand.

TERRY: Really?

JUNE: Sure, why not?

This is just what the banks did. Insurance companies like AIG were willing to write CDS insurance policies on some financial products, but not all. So banks wrote CDSs for each other. And they didn't just get CDSs for the stuff they owned. They also used CDSs to take side bets on the success or failure of the loans or bonds that other people owned. Side bets in sports may be illegal in much of America, but side bets in the financial markets are completely permissible. The law said nothing about how many CDS contracts that a bank could write, so the banks wrote billions of them, worth trillions of dollars in total.

These CDS contracts acted as mutual security for the banks. In a way, the banks were like mountain climbers, tying themselves together with these insurance contracts to keep each other safe. When mountaineers are climbing, they rope up together, so that if one climber falls over a

cliff, the combined weight and strength of rest of the party will hopefully save the fallen climber and prevent him from falling into the abyss. In the banks' case, rather than a single rope linking them up, the myriad contracts created a kind of spiderweb of connections, binding the Wall Street banks tightly together.

For almost a decade, all went well. The commercial and investment banks made money by the truckload, restrained only by the rickety, poorly policed barriers of the regulatory system, and protected by their bewildering network of CDS insurance policies. They turned into financial juggernauts that gobbled up business and squashed competitors all over the United States. But while they began to look identical on the surface, there was one important distinction between the investment banks and the big commercial banks.

The commercial banks, which included Citigroup, Chase Manhattan Bank, JP Morgan, Bank of America, and Wachovia, were also **retail banks**. Retail banks take deposits from customers and handle the paychecks of ordinary Americans. As a result, commercial banks are more heavily regulated than the investment banks, which back then included Goldman Sachs, Credit Suisse First Boston, Lehman Brothers, Bear Stearns, and Morgan Stanley. Because they handle the savings of ordinary Americans, commercial banks have to hold much more money in reserve for every loan they make. The upside of being a commercial bank is that they also have greater access to the Federal Reserve's lending facilities. They can tap the Federal Reserve for cash when things go wrong. And then there are the retail deposits in commercial banks' vaults. Those deposits can act as an enormous cushion if anything goes awry in the commercial bank's capital markets business.

Investment banks don't have those luxuries. If something goes wrong in an investment bank, it can't go to the Fed. That's the price it pays for being regulated much more lightly. Under normal circumstances, when disaster strikes at an investment bank and it needs cash, it has to go to another bank for help.

Banks on the Brink

The interbank lending market explored in chapter 7 is the beating heart of the banking system. Banks lend to consumers and corporations, but they also lend money to each other. They're happy to do so, as they believe that their fellow banks are normally among the safest bets in the market. The interbank lending market pumps the lifeblood of money from the center of the economy, the Federal Reserve, all the way out to the farthest extremities of the lending network, to local banks in Alaska or Hawaii.

Interbank lending is a big part of the banking business. Institutions lend money to each other for short periods, usually a week or less, or for just a few hours in the overnight market. This market between banks is highly liquid. There are always banks with a bit of extra cash to lend, and there are always banks that need a helping hand, for one reason or another. It's the same as in a human body, when different parts of the system require extra blood at certain times. Our legs demand more blood when we're running; our brain uses extra blood when we're concentrating; our thumbs suck up surplus blood when we're texting furiously on our BlackBerrys. The dollars pumping through the banking system are like the corpuscles pumping through our veins, and in both cases, there can be serious consequences when the supply to one part of the system is cut off.

It had never happened to anyone in the modern financial markets before, but on March 14, 2008, it happened to **Bear Stearns**. The investment bank had lost several billion dollars the previous summer, when two of its hedge funds collapsed. Since then, it had struggled to make a profit. The Bear hedge funds went under primarily because the bank made big bets on CDOs backed by mortgages that had turned out to be worthless. The damage done by the funds wasn't enough to sink Bear, but the other banks at the top of the system were nervous. They weren't just worried about Bear—they had all bought lots of CDOs, and it was beginning to dawn on them how toxic those investments might turn out to be. But no one knew just how much anyone else had bought, and how badly they might be affected.

So the banks began to demand more and more interest for overnight loans, and a **credit crunch** began to ripple through the American economy.

The Squeeze.

As interbank lending rates rose, banks naturally borrowed less from each other. That meant they had less money coming in the door, which meant they had less money going out the door. Less cash to invest, in other words, which meant fewer loans made to companies and consumers.

The Pinch.

As consumers found it more difficult to borrow money, they bought less stuff. Fewer cars, fewer houses, fewer clothes.

The Throttle.

Now the companies that made all that stuff were in trouble. On the one hand they were making less money from sales, and on the other hand, they couldn't borrow money from the banks, either because it was too expensive or because the banks weren't lending.

The Choke.

With less money coming in the door, companies had less cash to expand, buy inventory, and hire new people. So they stopped growing and began contracting. They laid people off, they closed stores, they shelved plans.

The Crunch.

And the economy began to grind to a halt.

It would take some time for Americans to realize how much danger they were in. But Bear Stearns knew immediately that it was in trouble. The bank was still struggling to contain the damage from the collapse of its two funds the summer before. Its other CDO investments were losing money as more and more Americans began to default on mortgages they never should have taken out. The other banks in the system could see all the damage reflected in Bear's quarterly statements, and they began to back away from Bear, demanding more and more in interest and collateral to lend to the troubled bank. Bear felt itself slipping away, as surely as if someone were slowly cutting off its blood supply.

And on the March 14, the banks stopped lending altogether.

If you cut off the blood flow to a limb, bad things begin to happen straightaway. The functioning parts of the limb shut down, one by one, and pretty soon the entire limb stops working altogether. And that's not the end of it. The body goes into shock, and the limb becomes infected. Necrosis and gangrene set in, and you're left with two options if you're to prevent infection spreading to the rest of the body. Either you get swift and radical medical attention, or you amputate.

Something similar happened to Bear Stearns. When the other banks refused to lend Bear any money, its operations began to fail. Because it couldn't borrow money, it couldn't lend money. Which meant it couldn't make money. Which meant it couldn't pay its bills. It transferred money from functioning parts of the business to other parts that owed money. But there simply wasn't enough cash left to go around.

As Bear began to collapse, panic set in. Bankers and regulators had two main concerns, both of which amounted to a kind of contagion. The first involved the web of CDS insurance contracts that bound all the banks to each other. Imagine the Wall Street skyscrapers, all bound together, perched on the edge of a cliff like a bunch of frozen, frightened mountaineers. As Bear Stearns began to topple toward the abyss, the banks began to worry that their CDS network protection scheme might not work, after all. Bear was so big and bound so tightly to the rest of the system that if it fell into the void, it might pull some or all of the other banks in with it. The answer was to unravel the ties holding them all together, but the network of credit default swaps was so complex and so dense, it was impossible to take it apart. For months, many banks had been betting that Bear would fail, and if it did, the people on the other sides of those bets would have to pay billions of dollars. Moreover, if Bear failed, how could it make either the monthly payments on securities that it had insured, or payouts on other bets that it had made with other banks? No one, not even the executives at Bear Stearns, knew the extent of the bank's liabilities.

The second fear of contagion involved the interbank lending system.

The banks began looking at each other, wondering which of them was the next Bear Stearns. Rates on overnight loans soared, and lending began to lock tighter and tighter. The secretary of the Treasury, Hank Paulson, and Ben Bernanke, the chairman of the Federal Reserve, feared that banks would soon stop lending to each other altogether. Many banks would then fail. Companies would go bankrupt. Unemployment would go through the roof. Earnings would go through the floor. The economy would go into reverse and a second Great Depression could result.

Stopping the Rot

Bernanke and Paulson considered their options. The way they saw it, allowing Bear to die would either drag the system down or make it grind to a halt, and that was unacceptable. Which meant they now had to wheel out the crash cart and start extraordinary measures to save the bank's life. They could have rescued the bank by simply giving it the money it needed, but that would have meant letting Bear get away with making stupid decisions and putting the entire financial system at risk. Paulson and Bernanke didn't want to let Bear Stearns fail, but they couldn't let the government be the savior. Moreover, they couldn't let Bear escape unpunished. So they decided to use a middleman. They convinced JPMorgan Chase to buy Bear Stearns and integrate it into JP Morgan's operations. And they lent JP Morgan the $30 billion it needed to do the deal. Bear Stearns had been a presence on Wall Street for eighty-seven years. But on March 16, the bank simply disappeared.

The markets breathed a sigh of relief. But there was no hiding the truth anymore. It was clear to everyone in the system that consumers had borrowed too much, and that banks had let them, and even helped them. Banks had borrowed too much, too, and regulators had waved them on. Everyone in the system had made big bets on housing, the biggest engine of the economic boom. Many banks and investors had bet far too much on securities they didn't understand, and which were now turning out to be worthless.

The demise—or rescue—of Bear didn't stop the cancer of fear from spreading through the financial system. The banks were still watching each other carefully and wondering who was next. The investment banks looked weakest, because they didn't have the deposits that the commercial banks had and they didn't have the same kind of access to the Federal Reserve that the commercial banks enjoyed. **Lehman Brothers** looked like the weakest investment bank of all. Like Bear, it had bet big on mortgage-backed CDOs, including on CDOs that it created itself. It took huge losses on the bonds in those CDOs and by the middle of August everyone could tell from Lehman's quarterly reports that the bank was in as much trouble as Bear had been six months earlier.

> Corporate America went astray largely because the power of managers went virtually unchecked by our gatekeepers for far too long. Our corporate directors were largely to blame. But our auditors, lawyers, regulators, legislators and investors, those other traditional guardians of sound governance, share the responsibility. They failed to "keep an eye on these geniuses" to whom they had entrusted the responsibility of the management of America's great corporations.
>
> **John C. Bogle, former CEO of the Vanguard Group, referring to the scandals at Enron and WorldCom. Bogle wrote this prescient passage in 2005, three years before the financial crisis that began in 2008.**

Once again, the other banks in the financial system began to back away. Lehman Brothers was still making a lot of money in many areas of its business, but at the same time it was losing so much money on its bad mortgage bets that those profits evaporated as soon as they

were made. The result was a **liquidity crisis**, which meant there simply wasn't enough money coming in the door to keep the company running. The only cash keeping the company afloat was the money it borrowed in the overnight market from other institutions. If Lehman could keep the interbank faucet open and keep that money flowing, it told the other banks, then it could make up for its losses by selling parts of its operations and building up its most profitable business lines. But the other banks weren't confident that Lehman knew how bad its bets were, or how much damage they might do. Lending money to Lehman suddenly looked unacceptably risky. So over the weekend of September 14, they turned the faucet off.

Again Paulson and Bernanke were faced with a decision: to save the Lehman limb or amputate it. They had "rescued" Bear, but they were worried that if they did the same with Lehman, other banks would indulge in **moral hazard**. Or, in other words, that they would continue taking big risks while assuming that the government would catch them in its safety net and bail them out. Treasury Secretary Paulson believed that moral hazard would poison the system. He figured the banks needed to learn the lesson that the government would not step in and rescue them after they had taken so much risk. There would be no crash cart for Lehman Brothers.

The company filed for bankruptcy on September 15, 2008.

Plundering the Public Purse

The stock market was already falling by this point. The collapse of Bear Stearns's two hedge funds in the summer of 2007 had showed Wall Street banks the dangers of the mortgage market, and they had stopped buying CDO bonds. That effectively shut down a lot of the shadow banking system, which in turn slowed securitization, cut off credit to consumers, put a brake on economic growth, and sent the stock market into reverse. But the collapse of Lehman Brothers sent the markets and the economy into a tailspin. The Dow Jones Industrial Average recorded its biggest drop since the 9/11 terror attacks, plunging 500 points, or about four and a half percent. At the same time, the interbank lending markets locked up, exactly as Paulson had feared might happen if Bear Stearns was allowed to fail. And as Lehman fell into the abyss, it began to drag the rest of Wall Street with it. One by one, the financial institutions collapsed or were taken over: AIG, Fannie Mae, Freddie Mac, Wachovia, Merrill Lynch, Washington Mutual.

> . . . the (2008 financial) crisis was not a natural disaster, but the result of high risk, complex financial products; undisclosed conflicts of interest; and the failure of regulators, the credit rating agencies, and the market itself to rein in the excesses of Wall Street.
>
> **"Wall Street and the Financial Crisis: Anatomy of a Financial Collapse," Permanent Subcommittee on Investigation, U.S. Senate, April 13, 2011**

As Ben Bernanke and Hank Paulson saw it, mortgages were at the root of the problem. Mortgages that irresponsible, avaricious lenders had made to unwitting or greedy people all over America; mortgages that were now worth nothing, because those borrowers couldn't make their interest payments; mortgages that had been bundled into CDOs, whose bonds were now worth next to nothing because so many of the mortgages in the bundles were worth nothing at all. Bad mortgages and their toxic CDO offspring were like a virus that was raging through the country, infecting every financial institution from the biggest banks in the nation to the smallest municipal pension funds. To Paulson and Bernanke, the only way to stop the infection was to cut it out immediately, and to take as many mortgages and CDOs off the banks' balance sheets as possible.

Within weeks of Lehman's collapse, the government announced the creation of the **Troubled Asset Relief Program**, a $700 billion fund to buy toxic debt from the banks. The idea was to **recapitalize** the banks, by injecting money into them and at the same time cutting some of the infection out. TARP was just the first of a slew of government programs aimed at getting the banks to lend to companies and consumers again.

Bernanke and Paulson's efforts appeared to save the economy, but the rescue came at an enormous cost. The government had to print trillions of dollars, loading the country with debt and putting the currency at enormous risk. But the price wasn't just financial. The bailout was proof that a number of banks had become so big that the government could not let them fail without threatening the entire financial system. Moral hazard, in other words, had become institutionalized. If you were too big to fail, then the government *had* to rescue you if things went wrong, so why not take as many risks as you liked?

Some politicians swore that banks would never again be allowed to become too big to fail. But it was too late for that. Rather than shrinking, in the days after the collapse of Lehman Brothers the banks had become even bigger. Bank of America gobbled up Merrill Lynch on September 14. JPMorgan Chase, which had already bought Bear Stearns, turned around and snapped up Washington Mutual less than two weeks

later. Wells Fargo bought Wachovia the following month. The demise of Lehman Brothers had nearly destroyed the market, yet Lehman was a pixie compared to these new behemoths of Wall Street. People could only imagine the devastation that the collapse of one of these financial juggernauts would wreak on the economy.

Many politicians and regulators were appalled by this prospect. Democratic senator Chris Dodd and Democratic representative Barney Frank decided they had to do as Democratic senators Carter Glass and Henry Steagall had done in the 1930s. Dodd and Frank drafted legislation that was signed into law in July 2010 as the **Wall Street Reform and Consumer Protection Act.** The act's supporters said it would usher in the greatest changes to financial regulation since the Great Depression.

The act has lofty ambitions, but there are some big differences between 1933 and 2010. For one thing, we already have a network of rules and regulations governing the financial markets and the banking system, something we didn't have in 1932. Our regulatory network may be as leaky as an old bucket and rather poorly policed, but it does exist. Hence the argument made by many people that we don't need more rules, just better administration of the regulation that's already in place.

Not everyone agrees with this point of view. Some say we need new rules to take into account the huge advances in technology that have transformed the markets. On the other side of the debating hall come the arguments that we should have fewer rules. An overcomplicated regulatory system inadvertently provides cover for rotten institutions and bad practices, they say. A small handful of good, properly enforced rules should do the job.

Neither side will win this debate entirely. The Dodd-Frank Act will be weaker than its authors proposed, and stronger than its opponents wish. When the ink has finally dried on the document, however, and we step back and look at our financial system, we will still see a system informed by the rule of law. We won't see an unfettered free market, where banks can dupe their customers without fear of consequence, or blithely game the system, secure in the knowledge that the government will catch them if they fall. The system won't be pretty, and it won't be perfect. It will have some big flaws, and it probably won't be equipped to cope with the next crisis, just as the Banking Act of 1933 didn't equip the system to cope with the effects of computerization and the exotic products of financial engineering. Looking back at history, we can pre-

dict with almost total certainty that our regulators and politicians will become complacent; banks will be allowed to become too big, and to behave in an overly aggressive way; consumers will overextend themselves. We will get ourselves into trouble. We will slip. We may well experience another crash. But by then, the seeds of our recovery will already have been sown.

AFTERWORD

Play a little word association game with anyone, and drop the word *market* in there, and your partner will likely respond with some kind of fruit or vegetable. Or maybe a fish! We're all familiar with what a market is. We know it's a place where people go to buy stuff. Or to sell it. The only difference between a financial market and your local fish market is that the product is less familiar.

But it's not the product that makes the market—it's the people doing the buying and selling. Without them, the market doesn't exist. In other words, markets are collections of people; they're communities. Whether the people in those communities are buying haddock or apples or bonds or credit default swaps, and whether they're buying and selling face-to-face in a trading pit, or using computer programs, they're all doing business to benefit themselves. But simply by participating in the market, they're helping sustain a place where anyone can go to do business, and that's beneficial for the entire community.

Because they're communities, markets have rules, even when the market is merely a bunch of people selling stuff out of the back of their cars in a windswept parking lot. But the rules are pretty basic. People can't sell stolen goods. And they can't sell poisonous or dangerous goods. Or stuff that's illegal. But otherwise, markets are pretty free. You can try to sell rotten fish if you want. Or wormy apples. The chances are, however, that the buyer will sniff you out and you won't sell a thing.

When it comes to financial markets, things get trickier. It's not that the markets themselves are any more complex: it's just a bunch of people buying and selling stuff, just like at the fish market. But the products are different in two ways. For one thing, buyers in the financial markets may not be familiar with the stuff that's on sale. It's a bit like a New Englander flying into a market in Singapore and trying to buy goods. What's this crazy-looking dragonfruit, and how do you eat it? What's this durian thing that looks like a cartoon dinosaur egg and smells so awful? In the financial markets, an entire industry has grown up around inventing exotic products that only the creators understand. They've conjured up an air of sophistication and mystery around these products and given them some mind-boggling names. That way, they've been able to corner the market in these products for themselves and justify the enormous salaries that they demand for dealing in them.

That's what this book is for—to demystify those markets. Just as a local guide and a little education can help our New Englander find her way around the Singaporean market—and avoid getting a stomachache—so a basic understanding of financial products can make the financial markets much more accessible to ordinary people.

But there is another reason why financial products are different from fruit and vegetables and fish. Buy a rotten fish or a fruit you're not familiar with and you may get sick for a while. Buy a dodgy financial product and you could end up doing serious damage to your savings, impacting your life beyond just a day or two. If you're a banker managing other people's portfolios, buying a toxic product could trash the accounts you manage and ruin all of your clients' lives. In other words, making poor or ill-informed decisions with financial products can have enormous repercussions, and can affect a great many people, which is why governments put so many rules in place governing the financial markets. There will always be disagreement about how many rules there should be, and how far they should reach, and we'll never find the "right" balance. The important thing is that we have the debate in the first place. Simply allowing the financial markets to work as freely as a car trunk sale is too dangerous, given the effects that financial products can have. But at the same time, tying the markets up in red tape can have a stifling effect and make it hard to do business.

Finding the Goldilocks amount of regulation in the financial markets requires knowledge and understanding. That knowledge and understanding can only be acquired if the markets are demystified. We've seen how the elevation of the financial markets to a higher plane can damage an economy; and how the exaltation of traders and bankers can divide a nation. The only way to prevent this is to get politicians and the people who elect them to learn how these markets work and what the people who pull the levers and push the switches actually do. Once we understand that the goings-on down on Wall Street are not the practice of some kind of black art, then we can make a start at building the kind of markets that benefit all of us and no longer represent a threat.

INDEX

ABOUT THE AUTHOR

Paddy Hirsch is a senior producer at American Public Media's business radio program production house, *Marketplace*. He is the creator of the acclaimed and popular *Marketplace* Whiteboard, which was a Webby honoree in 2009, and has been featured on network and public broadcast television. He recently completed a Knight Fellowship in Journalism at Stanford University. Hirsch lives in Los Angeles, California.